D1169024

# Rock Your World

how
you
can
make a
difference

## Susie Shellenberger

Barefoot Ministries
Kansas City, Missouri

ISBN 083-415-0018

Printed in the United States of America

Editor: James K. Hampton

Cover Design: Doug Bennett

The author and publisher gratefully acknowledge the use of the following previously published articles that have been adapted for this book:

"On Fire in Florida" by Michael Ross, *Breakaway* magazine, Vol. 8, No. 11, November 1997, published by Focus on the Family. Copyright © 1997, Focus on the Family. All rights used. International copyright secured. Used by permission.

"God's Gifts Are the Best" by Susie Shellenberger, *Brio* magazine, Vol. 9, No. 2, February 1998, published by Focus on the Family. Copyright © 1998, Focus on the Family. All rights reserved. International copyright secured. Used by permission.

"Earth Facts" by Susan M. Stevens. Used by permission of the author.

"Just Kids" by Nina C. Pykare. Used by permission of the author.

"Cross-Cultural Connection" by Sarah Meekhof. Used by permission of the author.

Published in association with the literary agency of Alive Communications, Inc., 7680 Goddard Street, Suite 200, Colorado Springs, Colorado, 80920.

# table of Contents

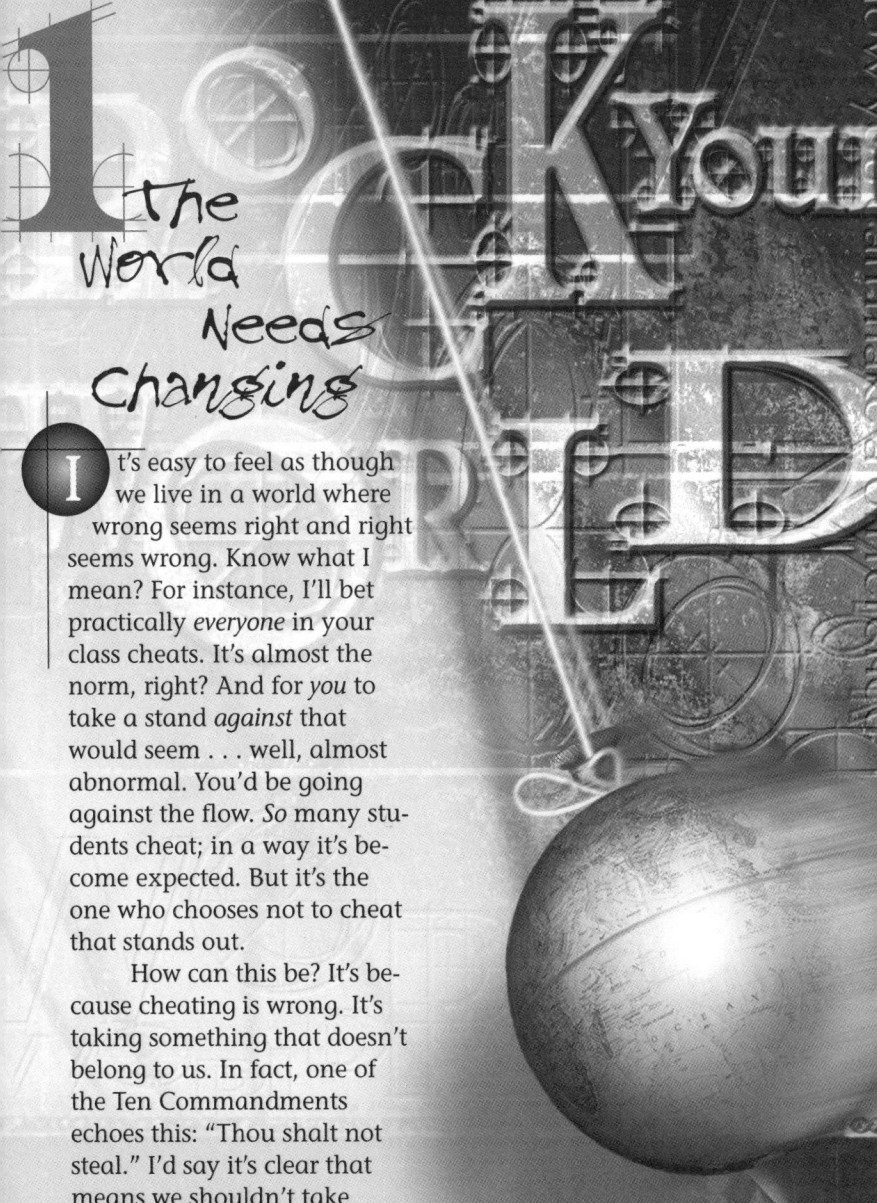

# 1

## LOCK Your World

### The World Needs Changing

I t's easy to feel as though we live in a world where wrong seems right and right seems wrong. Know what I mean? For instance, I'll bet practically *everyone* in your class cheats. It's almost the norm, right? And for *you* to take a stand *against* that would seem . . . well, almost abnormal. You'd be going against the flow. *So* many students cheat; in a way it's become expected. But it's the one who chooses not to cheat that stands out.

How can this be? It's because cheating is wrong. It's taking something that doesn't belong to us. In fact, one of the Ten Commandments echoes this: "Thou shalt not steal." I'd say it's clear that means we shouldn't take something that doesn't belong to us, wouldn't you? Yet, *somehow* over the years, we've broken the rules. And somehow, what's wrong doesn't seem so wrong anymore.

5

*You're Not Alone*

If you're committed to taking a stand against sin (including cheating), you are probably feeling outnumbered. And even though it may *feel* like you're standing alone, you're not.

Compromise, sin, and breaking the rules have been around messing up this world for a long time. Check out what the prophet Isaiah said almost a bazillion years ago: "Our courts oppose the righteous man; fairness is unknown. Truth falls dead in the streets, and justice is outlawed" (Isaiah 59:14, TLB).

Sound like a fair description of our world today? We sometimes feel as though our judicial system has gone bonkers, good people aren't treated fairly, and not a single person knows what truth is—or even cares about finding it.

Why do we feel this way about the world we are living in? Maybe it's because a thousand voices are screaming their own philosophies, opinions, alternative lifestyles, and ideas at us. And when those voices clearly shout the *opposite* of what God's Word teaches, it's tempting to sit down instead of stand up. It's also easy to become confused.

Does any of this sound familiar? According to TV, magazines, advertising, and popular culture, it's OK (and sometimes expected) to

- dress provocatively to arouse interest from the opposite sex.

- engage in sexual intercourse outside of marriage (as long as you use protection).
- drink (as long as you don't drink and drive).

- sexually experiment with the same sex (just to know what it's like).
- bend the truth, deceive, or lie if the situation calls for it.

- abort the "mistake" if you get pregnant and don't want to clutter your life.

Even though all of the above clearly go against the Bible, we're tempted to think, "it's OK" simply because "everyone else is doing it." The truth is, not everyone else is doing it. But we'll talk about that in few minutes, OK?

Ultimately, you have a decision to make. You have to decide who you're going to listen to. And you're not the only one making this decision. Jehoshaphat, a very cool king from the Old Testament, had to make the same decision.

The stage for this story is set in 2 Chronicles 17 and 18. Lots of action! Jehoshaphat was known as a godly man and a wise king. *But* his friend King Ahab was *not* a godly man. He wanted power, power, and more power. Pretty selfish, huh?

He decided he'd like to expand his land by conquering another city—Ramoth-gilead. (That's a mouthful. How would like to write *that* on all your envelopes? We'll just call it RG for short.) When Ahab asked Jehoshaphat if he'd support him in war against RG, Jehoshaphat gave a smart answer: "Let's check with the Lord first" (2 Chronicles 18:4, TLB).

So King Ahab summoned 400 of his prophets. They were people who *sounded* good (maybe like some talk show hosts you've heard), *looked* good (maybe like some celebrities you've seen), and *acted* right (maybe like some friends of yours), but they weren't committed to God's Lordship.

These 400 prophets were enthusiastic! They held a giant pep rally, made up "RG cheers," and handed out friendship bracelets to everyone who supported them. They screamed to King Ahab in unison, "Go ahead, for God will give you a great victory!" (2 Chronicles 18:5, TLB).

But Jehoshaphat wasn't convinced. It wasn't that he didn't *want* a friendship bracelet; they were awesome. The problem was that he didn't hear God's voice among the prophets.

You'd think 400 good people all shouting the same good message would be enough, wouldn't you? After all, they were so positive and enthusiastic! They sounded good, looked good, and acted good.

But Jehoshaphat stood alone. He had asked for a godly prophet. It's like he was saying, "It's tempting to believe the celebrities. I'm really impressed. *But* I'm listening for God's voice, and you know what? I don't hear it! Even with 400 good prophets sending 400 good messages that sound tempting, I'm still not able to discern God's voice."

He asked again for a godly prophet. "Isn't there some prophet of the Lord around here too?" he asked. "I'd like to ask him the same question" (2 Chronicles 18:6, TLB).

King Ahab squirmed and cleared his throat. "Well, yeah. There *is* this one guy. But I don't like listening to him. The stuff he says isn't always fun to hear. His name is Micaiah. Bring him in."

## The Tension Builds

Micaiah was prompted before he was brought to the king. One of the servants warned him that the other 400 prophets had already encouraged Ahab to go to war. "If you know what's good for you, you'll do the same," he pressed.

But when Micaiah was brought before the king, he spoke the truth. He explained that the Lord had put a lying spirit in the mouths of the 400 prophets, and that they were actually telling him to go against God's will—even though it appeared to be a godly message!

Hmmm. Sound like our culture today? We're literally bombarded by thousands of screaming voices that may *sound* good, but unless those voices agree with the Word of God, they are deceptive, dangerous, and full of lies.

So, choose your pep rallies with caution and decide very carefully to whom you'll choose to listen. It isn't always the enthusiastic voice that conveys truth. Rather, it is the Voice that speaks through the Bible, your heart, your pastor, and other spiritual leaders that ultimately proclaims the truth.

# Digging Deeper

Let's start digging in to *truth*. When we hear so many different voices screaming so many different things, how can we *really know* what's right and what's wrong?

If you've accepted Jesus Christ as Lord of your life, you're basing your lifestyle and your thoughts around His Holy Word. The catch? Just this: Is He *really* Lord?

Did you know "Lord" is mentioned 7,540 times in the Bible? Hmmm. God must think it's pretty important, huh? "Lord" means one who has control. He is the one who has absolute authority.

It's God's will that we live under the *Lordship* of His Son, Jesus Christ. Bottom line: It means He is Boss! He is the supreme controller of the universe.

In John 13:13, we see that the disciples addressed Him as Lord. They probably called Him Jesus, too, but when they *addressed* Him, it was Lord.

Remember that violent storm on the Sea of Galilee? (You can find the whole story in Matthew 14:22-32.) The disciples—grown men of whom some were professional seamen—were scared to death! Peter screamed, "Lord! If it's You, ask me to come to You." Even in fear, he referred to Jesus as Lord.

And after Christ had broken out of His grave clothes, conquered death, and escaped the tomb, the women who went looking for Him declared, "They have taken our Lord." Not Jesus. Not the Messiah. But *Lord*.

So? What's all of this leading to? Stick with me, OK? We'll wind up at *truth* in a minute. And *that* will help you discern to whom and to what to listen. But first we've gotta go down the right road to get there.

# What's It All Mean?

Jesus Christ wants to be much more than number one in your life. Being number one isn't good enough. He wants to be your life. You see, He knows that whatever or whoever we place at the number one position in our lives can eventually get shoved to the number two spot. Or number three. Or four.

We always talk about Jesus living in our hearts. But guess what? He doesn't want to settle for just your heart. He wants to live in your mind too. He wants to permeate your being. He wants to possess your thoughts but not control you like a puppet. He doesn't work that way. But He wants to possess your thinking in such a way that the things that break His heart will also break your heart. And the atrocities that bring tears to Christ's eyes will make you cry. And the injustices that cause *Him* to stand in righteous anger will cause *you* to stand in righteous anger.

He wants you to be *saturated* with Him. To be almost obsessed with becoming all He calls you to be. We're not talking about ordinary Christianity, are we? Nope, we're talking about an intense commitment. A holy focus. A godly mindset. We're talking about *Lordship.*

## The Call

Jesus Christ *begs* you to move away from casual Christianity. The world is filled with too many weak-kneed, wishy-washy Christians. He has a much higher calling on your life, and He asks for a much deeper commitment from you. He wants your all! He wants to be your Lord.

You see, He's interested in every single area of your life. The big stuff *and* the little stuff. He wants to be involved in your friendships, your dating life, your extracurricular activities, your part-time job, your family, your dreams, your fears, your celebrations, your *everything*. Why? Because that's what Lordship is all about. Is God nosy? Well, maybe a little bit, but it's because He loves you more than you'll ever imagine. And this is why He wants all of you. We're often tempted to say, "Yeah, OK. You can be Lord. But stay out of what I buy. Don't get involved in how I use my free time." But when we're sick, or our back is up against the wall, we call on Him. We want to choose when He's Lord.

But this full commitment we're talking about won't work that way. You see, Jesus didn't come just to save us. He also came to master us, to break us and reshape us in His image, and to empower our lives in order to bring glory to Him.

Whew! That's a high calling. But Jesus *invites* us to participate in the highest calling imaginable—to make Him Lord. And we're talking Lord of *all.*

And if you so choose, this decision will affect every aspect of your life: How you dress, the jokes you tell, the stuff you watch, and what you listen to. Oh, you'll still make mistakes—that's what grace is all about. But the difference is that you're changing your *focus.* And you're allowing Jesus to break and reshape your heart, your desires, and your will.

## What About It?

So, I'm wondering. Who will take their dreams, their relationships, their talents, their future, their attitudes, their *all,* and pray, "Jesus, I'm Yours. You have permission to break me and reshape me into all You dream for me to be. I even give You the stuff I don't know about yet—the stuff that will happen in the future. I don't want to settle for casual Christianity. I do *not* want a surface-level relationship with You. I want *all* of You. And I want You to have all of *me.* Take me, Father. Fill me, saturate me, permeate me with Your Spirit, Your power. Energize me. Guide me. Take me where You want me to go. Tell me what You want me to do. I'm here to bring glory to You."

Who will do that? I know a 17-year-old girl from Germantown, Tennessee, who's doing just that. Laura Robertson asks herself the question, "What would Jesus do?" before everything she does. And you know what? It's changed her life.

"Sometimes I'm sitting at home on Friday nights instead of going out with my friends," she says. "They may go see a movie that I know Jesus wouldn't want me to see. But you know what? It's OK! The rewards in my life and the spiritual growth that He's brought are simply incredible! It's worth far, far more than missing a movie every now and then."

What will happen if you ask that question? If *you* pray that prayer of Lordship? Well, things will change. Not only your lifestyle, but your thinking too. Even how you see truth. Speaking of truth, that's what we were talking about way back in the beginning, wasn't it? Hmmm. Well, let's tackle it in the next chapter. Don't worry. I'll make that part short so we can hurry up and get into more real-life stories from dedicated teens like Laura, OK?

# 2

## I Believe

**LOCK Your WORLD**

**L**et's repeat a couple of things from the first chapter, OK?

*When we hear so many different voices that scream so many different things, how can we really know what's right and what's wrong?*

*If you've accepted Jesus Christ as Lord of your life, you're basing your lifestyle and your thoughts around His Holy Word. The catch? Just this: Is He really Lord?*

If you've decided to truly make Jesus *Lord*—to give Him complete, absolute control—then you'll also accept His Holy Word, the Bible, as truth. And when you, in turn, accept Him as Truth, you're ready to influence—even *change*—the world around you.

I have chosen to believe that Jesus really *is* who He claims to be—the Son of the living God. The One who created the universe. The One who died for my sins, rose from the dead, lives today, hears my prayers, gives me wisdom and discernment, strengthens me, and enables me to live a godly life. I believe the Bible is His inspired Word of truth. And therefore, I believe He is Truth.

Check *this* out: "I am the Way—yes, and the Truth and the Life. No one can get to the Father except by means of me" (John 14:6, TLB).

Not only does Jesus tell us that He is Truth; He also warns us that no one can come to God without going through Him. Hmmm. Know what that shows us? It shows that a lot of people who *call* themselves Christians really aren't living the Christian life. It shows us that many are accepting what the media and our culture say is truth, when it's really not truth at all.

In fact, we read in Acts 20:30 that men will distort the truth. And in the Book of 1 John, we're warned that there are many false teachers around (people who claim that what they say is true and biblical when actually it goes against God's Word).

---

So What?

So it might get tough to be a sold-out, deeply committed Christian going against the flow. *But* we should expect that! In fact, we've already been warned: "In the last days it is going to be very difficult to be a Christian" (2 Timothy 3:1, TLB). Paul goes on to warn Timothy that these people will go to church but won't live by godly preaching. And even though they *say* they speak truth, they really don't even *understand* it, because they haven't accepted Jesus as the ultimate Truth.

I've listened to those people on TV, haven't you? I've heard talk show hosts convince their audiences that it's OK to lie, sleep around, and pretty much do whatever you want—as long as you're careful and you try not to hurt others. I've even heard *some* of these celebrities refer to themselves as Christians.

But guess what? If what they're saying doesn't jive with what *God* says in the Bible, they're phonies. Fakes. False prophets.

The apostle John tells us how to handle this kind of message: "Dearly loved friends, don't always believe everything you hear just because someone says it is a message from God: test it first to see if it really is. For there are many false teachers around" (1 John 4:1, TLB). John then challenges us to see if the messages we're hearing stack up against the Bible. Does it agree with what God says? Or does it go against God's Word? That's how we can discern if what we're hearing is truth. Again, once you've tapped into God's Word as the ultimate truth, He'll equip you with the power, wisdom, and discernment you need to influence—even change—the world around you.

---

## She Knows the Truth

Seventeen-year-old Melissa Wagner knows the truth. She's a committed Christian who has accepted God's Word as the ultimate authority in her life. It's one thing to know and accept the truth, but it's quite another thing to act on it—especially when it means going against the flow of the culture around you.

Melissa lives right outside of Chicago, and her dad is a pastor in the area. Since they live close to the Windy City, her mom always thought it would be fun to visit the Oprah Winfrey show. She made the necessary arrangements, got tickets, and took Melissa with her.

"It was practically an all-day thing," Melissa remembers. "We had to line up outside Harpo Studios around 7:30 A.M."

The crowd was finally directed inside to sit in the studio audience for the taping of *Oprah*. Melissa and her mom had no idea what the show would be about that day. They were just excited to be there.

Before the show actually started, the director came out and chatted with the audience. "How many of you are here for the first time?" he asked. Melissa, her mom, and several others raised their hands.

"We're glad to have you," he responded. "And we're really excited about today's taping!"

"Now before we get rolling, let me fill you in on what will be happening. As many of you know, Oprah professes to be a devout Christian. Today's show will be centered on her guest appearance as a therapist on the *Ellen* show. On it, she will encourage Ellen to declare her homosexuality. Anyone have a problem with that?"

While the majority of the audience smiled and clapped, Melissa squirmed uncomfortably in her seat. *Wait a second,* she thought. *The Bible is very clear on homosexuality. Is Oprah going to contradict God's Word?*

The director eyed the studio audience as Melissa glanced at her mom.

"That's not right," she said. "I can't just sit here." She slowly stood to her feet, climbed over several people in her aisle, and approached the microphone that was set up on one side of the audience.

"I do," she said softly into the microphone, which amplified her words to the Oprah fans around her.

"You do what?" asked the director.

"Well, you asked if anyone had a problem with that," she said. "And I do."

"Oh, is that so?" he queried. "Why?"

"Well," Melissa began. "If Oprah really *is* a devout Christian, how can she blatantly go against the Bible? If she's a devout Christian, she's gotta accept God and all that He says as the ultimate truth."

"Would you be willing to say that on national television?" the director pressed.

"I . . . I guess so," she answered.

And . . . . ACTION!

The lights flashed, cameras moved back and forth, someone shouted last-minute directions to a crewmember, the music began, and Oprah, the queen of daytime talk, appeared on stage.

After warming up the audience, she announced the direction that she would be taking with today's show.

"I'm told someone here has a problem with me guest-starring on Ellen's show," she said. "Melissa, where are you?"

Melissa stood and faced the microphone again. "Melissa, I understand that you're a Christian," Oprah began.

"Yes," Melissa answered.

"I am too. We serve the same God. What's your beef with me

appearing in the role of a therapist on *Ellen* and encouraging her to declare her homosexuality?"

"It goes against the Bible," Melissa stated. "It seems you're contradicting yourself—saying you're a Christian but not accepting His Word as the ultimate truth."

"Melissa, the God I serve loves everybody—heterosexuals and homosexuals."

"Sure He does," she began. "But—"

And Oprah cut her off. While others in the audience verbalized their support of advocating homosexuality on prime-time television, Melissa remained by the microphone, trying to complete her thought.

"Yes, He asks us to love everyone—"

And again, Oprah cut her off. Time after time, throughout the entire show, Oprah badgered Melissa—accusing her of being narrow-minded and intolerant.

As the show was nearing the end, Melissa continued to stand her ground by the microphone. "I started crying," she remembers. "Not because they were giving me a hard time, but because Oprah just doesn't get it. My heart goes out to her. She's deceived."

Oprah called Melissa's name again, reminding her and the rest of her worldwide viewers that God is a God of love and that He loves *everybody.*

The camera zoomed in on Melissa who was standing tall with tears streaming down her face. "But . . . that doesn't mean that . . . that . . . we have to accept their *lifestyle,*" she stammered.

And Oprah cut her off.

The theme music faded in as the cameras pulled back. The queen of daytime talk waved good-bye and smiled big to her fans.

It was a strong picture: A 17-year-old girl standing up to Oprah Winfrey with tears running down her cheeks. Over the next few weeks, Oprah replayed that clip during a series of shows covering homosexuality.

But *Oprah* was not the only show. Several other stations, including CNN, picked up the clip and began airing it on *their* airwaves.

*What a way to make a national television debut,* Melissa thought.

## The Heat Still Rises

Standing up to Oprah was hard, but it wasn't the toughest obstacle Melissa would face. The next few days at school were a nightmare.

"It was awful," she remembers. "Even some of my Christian friends turned against me.

"They said stuff like, 'Well, homosexuality might be wrong for you, but who are you to say it's wrong for someone else?' What are they thinking? The Bible says it's wrong for *everyone.*"

Because Melissa Wagner is committed to the *Lordship* of Jesus Christ, she has accepted His Word as the ultimate truth, and now she lives her life by it. She's allowing Him to permeate every area of her being. And because she knows truth, God is using her to influence the world around her.

Guess what? When *you* know God as absolute Truth, He'll use *you* to change the world. Think about it: He could have chosen anyone to confront Oprah Winfrey. (People such as Billy Graham, James Dobson, or Chuck Swindoll would have been a great choice.)

But instead, He empowered a 17-year-old girl, plugged into extraordinary power, to stop Oprah in her tracks and make her think.

## Just Between Us

You may be thinking, *Wait a second! I thought that as Christians we are supposed to accept everyone. I'm not sure I'm tracking with you. I have non-Christian friends who are living in sin. I can't just dump them. And I'm not sure God would want me to.*

Good point. Glad you jumped in. Before we actually get into how we can change our world, let's chat first, OK? Just you and me. (See, when you write a book, you switch directions, interrupt yourself, ask questions, and basically go anywhere you want. Cool, huh?)

God commands us to love *everyone.* In fact, love is one major way the world can see that Christians are different. Take a look at these verses on love:

"And so I am giving a new commandment to you now—love each other just as much as I love you. Your strong love for each other will prove to the world that you are my disciples" (John 13:34-35, TLB).

And get this: "Little children, let us stop just *saying* we love people; let us *really* love them, and *show it* by our actions" (1 John 3:18, TLB).

Memorize this: "If anyone says 'I love God,' but keeps on hating his brother, he is a liar; for if he doesn't love his brother who is right there in front of him, how can he love God whom he has never seen? And God himself has said that one must love not only God, but his brother too" (1 John 4:20-21, TLB).

## So, What's It Mean?

*Yeah. That's what I'm talking about. Love. If we're supposed to love everyone, how can you come on so strongly against stuff?*

While God calls us to love everyone, including sinners, He never asks us to love a sinful lifestyle. In other words, He wants us to love the sinner and hate the sin.

*But I thought as Christians we were supposed to be tolerant.*

You're right—to a point.

## We're to be tolerant in:

- not demanding to be first.

- not always assuming our opinions are right (notice I said *opinions*—which are different from what's written in the Bible).
- listening to those around us.

- accepting everyone—regardless of race, beliefs, or physical attributes.
- allowing others to express their views.

In these areas, tolerance is definitely a virtue (meaning, a real good thing; a characteristic to be desired). But tolerance isn't *always* a virtue! Let's look at our example: Jesus loved everyone, but He didn't tolerate sin. Remember when He chased the moneychangers right out of the temple? Another time, He got so angry at sin that He cursed a fig tree, and it withered. He called some folks, who *claimed* to be godly people, hypocrites.

See, tolerance doesn't mean accepting everything. It *does* mean accepting people. But as sold-out disciples committed to His Lordship, we have to draw the line at accepting (or being tolerant of) sin.

Tolerance applies only to persons and never to truth! Tolerance applies to the erred and intolerance to the error. We must be tolerant with people but *intolerant* where truth is at stake. We can't afford to compromise what the Bible says is wrong and become tolerant of those who rationalize it as right. Sin is *always* sin.

*So Melissa's Christian friends, who gave her a hard time, were sort of copping out, weren't they?*

They sure were! You're listening to dangerous rhetoric anytime you hear someone say, "Well, maybe it's wrong for me, but I can't say it's wrong for someone else."

Like I mentioned before, sin is sin. What the Bible says is wrong for *me* is also wrong for you.

*But when we put it that way, doesn't it make us sound judgmental?*
Yeah, it probably does. But sometimes it's OK to judge.
*Huh?*
Let's sneak a peek at what the apostle Paul has to say about it:

"When I wrote to you before I said not to mix with evil people. But when I said that I wasn't talking about unbelievers who live in sexual sin, or are greedy cheats and thieves and idol worshipers. For you can't live in this world without being with people like that. What I meant was that you are not to keep company with anyone who claims to be a brother Christian but indulges in sexual sins, or is greedy, or is a swindler, or worships idols, or is a drunkard, or abusive. Don't even eat lunch with such a person.

"It isn't our job to judge outsiders. But it certainly is our job to judge and deal strongly with those who are members of the church, and who are sinning in these ways" *(1 Corinthians 5:9-12, TLB)*.

In other words, it's *always* OK to call sin "sin." It's OK to be intolerant of sin. We don't have to accept it—we're not *supposed* to accept it. Paul encourages us not to hang out with people who *say* they're Christians but don't abide by God's Truth.

When it comes to sin and truth and the compromising of God's Holy Word, it's OK to be narrow-minded. After all, we *should* be walking a straight and narrow road.

*Makes sense. OK. I accept the Bible as truth. And I'm committed to the Lordship of Jesus Christ. But seriously, how can God use me to make a difference? To initiate change?*

Glad you asked. Keep reading.

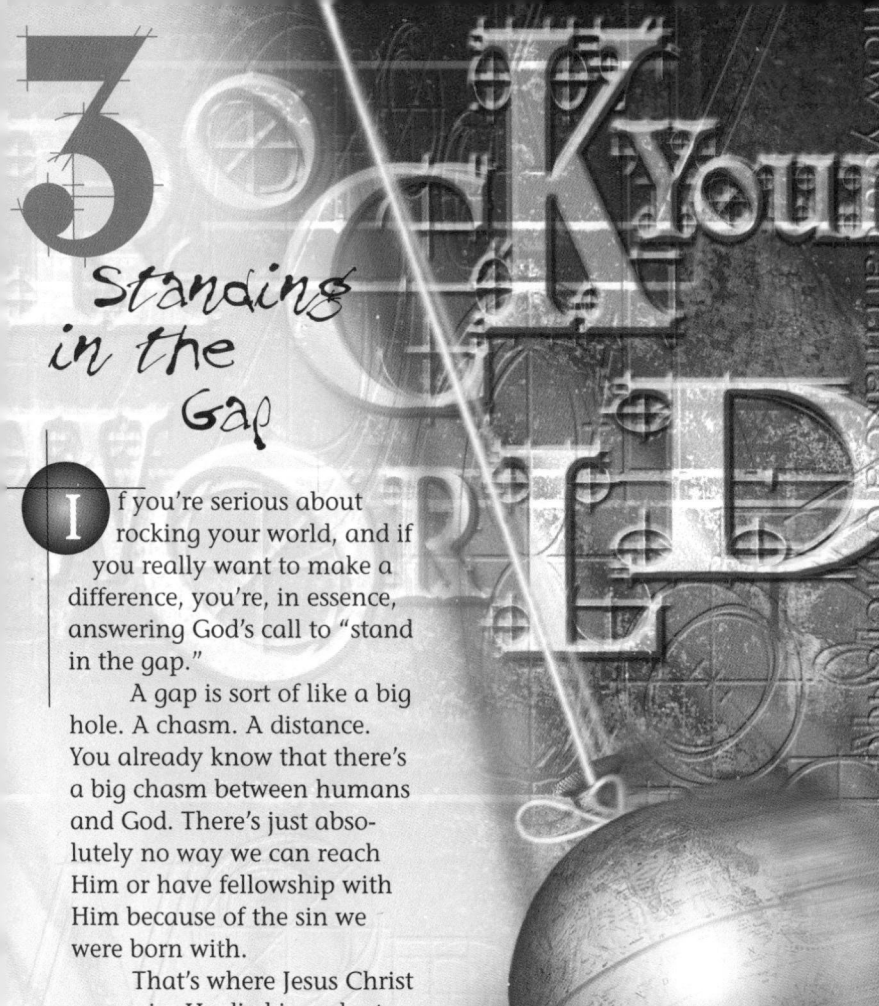

# 3

## Standing in the Gap

I f you're serious about rocking your world, and if you really want to make a difference, you're, in essence, answering God's call to "stand in the gap."

A gap is sort of like a big hole. A chasm. A distance. You already know that there's a big chasm between humans and God. There's just absolutely no way we can reach Him or have fellowship with Him because of the sin we were born with.

That's where Jesus Christ comes in. He died in order to be the bridge. Through *Him,* we can have an intimate relationship with God. Jesus fills in the hole. He stands in the gap. He becomes our connection to a holy God.

But guess what? He asks *us* to do the same! He's calling *you* to stand in the gap, fill in the hole, and bridge the chasm between a lost and dying world and an eternity with the Father.

This exciting call is spelled out specifically in Ezekiel 22:30: "I looked in vain for anyone who would stand in the gap, but I found not one" (author's paraphrase).

God is looking desperately for *anyone* to stand in the gap. *Anyone?* Anyone! That means you don't have to qualify, try out, or audition. There won't be any callbacks. You don't have to be good enough, smart enough, pretty enough, handsome enough, athletic enough, rich enough, or popular enough. He's looking for *anyone!* And that anyone is you—*if* you're willing to answer the call.

## What Does It Mean?

Standing in the gap means being a human bridge, a connector, between those around you and Jesus Christ. Being a bridge means you're going to get walked on. Standing in the gap isn't always easy. It requires commitment and sacrifice. It will cost you.

I recently flew from Northern California to Los Angeles and from there to Oklahoma City. When I debarked from my flight in Los Angeles, I noticed a foreign woman behind me who was frazzled and frightened. I couldn't understand her because she was speaking a language I didn't know.

Even though I was unable to decipher her words, it was obvious she was trying to figure out where to go. She didn't understand what her ticket said and didn't have a clue about the huge Los Angeles International airport. No one was helping her. Even the flight attendants seemed oblivious to her needs!

I didn't have much time between connections and didn't want to miss my flight to Oklahoma City, so I turned to rush toward my gate. But God checked me, "Wait a minute, Susie. I thought you made a commitment to stand in the gap."

"Well, yeah. I did, God. But I've gotta make this flight."

"But *no one* is helping her! She's my daughter. I need *you* to stand in the gap for her."

"But . . ."

"Be a bridge, Susie. Make the connection for her. Stand in the gap."

I turned around and caught her attention. Then I motioned for her to follow me. I took her to the monitor listing the departing and returning flights, and after looking at her ticket, I found her gate listing.

"43 B," I said. "You go to 43 B."

Well, obviously, she didn't understand what I was saying. I checked my watch, swallowed, grabbed her hand, and started running through the airport. What a sight! Two ladies, hand-in-hand, dashing between people, electric carts, baby strollers, and security guards, headed straight for gate 43 B.

We finally arrived. I knew she wouldn't understand my English, so I tried to act out my words as I spoke. "You (I pointed at her) go here (I pointed toward the gate). You fly away (I flapped my arms like a bird). I took her to the check-in desk and watched her smile for the first time since I'd seen her. A wave of relief seemed to wash over her as she realized she was in the right place—and at the right time.

I waved good-bye and tore through the airport once again. I arrived at the gate for my Oklahoma City departure, but, I guess in all of the running, I must have dropped my ticket. I couldn't find it anywhere!

I begged the airline employee to let me board the plane. "You can punch me up on the computer," I said. "It'll show you that I really *am* a passenger on this flight, and that I really *do* have a ticket, and that it really *has* been paid for!"

"Yes, I can see that," he responded. "But I can't let you board this plane without a ticket and boarding pass in your hand. You'll have to run down to the terminal and purchase a new ticket."

I thought I had run fast to gate 43 B with my new friend. And I broke *that* speed running to my Oklahoma City gate. But now, dashing all the way to the terminal and back, I'm pretty sure I broke an Olympic record (if you don't count the tourists I downed en route).

If you've flown before, you know that purchasing a one-way ticket on the day of departure is not cheap. I charged a ticket from Los

Angeles to Oklahoma City that I really couldn't afford. And when I arrived at the gate, right before they shut the door to the plane, I crashed into seat 18 C and pulled the seat belt across my waist.

And then it happened. God spoke. Ever so softly, ever so sure.

"It cost you didn't it, Susie?"

"Sure did. God, I can't afford—"

"Don't ever second-guess it if it was worth it. It cost you. But Susie, it cost *Me* a whole lot more to stand in the gap for *you.*"

I've never second-guessed it since. I've struggled with it—but never second-guessed it.

---

## You're Not Alone

Even though it may *seem* like you stand in the gap alone, you really don't. Jesus promised He'd always be with us! There are times you'll stand humanly alone, but there is *never* a time when He's not with you!

A couple of years ago, I was in Uganda, Africa, with Compassion International. I was at a school and noticed a 14-year-old girl in the distance. Other girls her age were pushing her back and forth on the swings. Even from across the schoolyard, I could hear her squeals of laughter. I watched as she jumped out of the swing and ran a short distance to start playing kick the can with some other kids. It was obvious she had a lot of friends. I kept my eyes on her for most of the day. Kids were always around her. She never stopped smiling.

But there was something different about this young teen. She had no arms. I found the schoolmaster and pointed toward the girl. "Tell me about her," I said. "What's her story?"

His face lit up like a proud papa. "Oh, that's Rose," he said. "When she was an infant, a wild pig ran into her village and ate her arms. Her mother was so repulsed, she took Rose a few miles outside of the village and abandoned her on a dirt road. A Christian found her, took her to a clinic, and made arrangements for her to be adopted. She's my daughter. My wife and I adopted her when she was about a year old."

Wow. What a fantastic way to stand in the gap! This young man and his wife are being the bridge for Rose. They're making a difference. It's not easy to raise a girl with no arms. They've had to teach her to eat, dress, and do everyday tasks that the rest of us don't think twice about. It's costing them. They're making a sacrifice. But they're also making a lifetime difference for a girl who could have otherwise been stuck in an orphanage her whole life.

## BUT HOW DO I DO IT?

Standing in the gap begins with commitment—a simple decision to answer the call of God on your life. If we're really going to claim that Jesus is Lord, standing in the gap is not optional. It's nonnegotiable. It's something we do in radical obedience to Him.

So, how about it? Are you ready to make a promise? A lifetime pledge to make a difference by standing in the gap? Hopefully this isn't just one more promise or another casual, emotional decision. Hopefully it's a pledge, a commitment, a *resolve* that will affect the rest of your life. In other words, because of this sacred oath, you will never be the same. You'll be tuned in to, and intensely focused on, being a bridge, making a difference, standing in the gap, and being Jesus to those around you.

Yes, it costs to stand in the gap. It's hard sometimes. It's not always popular and it doesn't always make sense. But we don't stand in the gap just because everyone else is. Because the truth is, everyone else *isn't*. We don't stand in the gap because it's cool. It's sometimes lonely and frustrating. No, we stand in the gap because Jesus stood in the gap for us.

And because He stood in the gap for us, we, in turn, stand in the gap for each other. Ephesians 5:1 tells us to imitate our Father. That means standing in the gap. Being a bridge. Getting walked on. It isn't always easy, but it is always right.

Oh, yeah, one more thing. There *are* rewards. We just don't have room in this book to list them all! Well, OK, I'll list one. Flip to the next chapter and read about a teen girl who sacrificed something very important and got back more than she could have ever imagined!

But, wait! Before you turn to the next chapter, how 'bout making a "standing in the gap" pledge? If that's your heart's desire, I invite you to pray this prayer:

*"Father, I don't want to settle for casual Christianity. I want to be all You've created me to be. I want to stand in the gap and be used by You. I want to make a difference in my world. I realize it will not be easy. I know it will cost me. I'll have to make sacrifices. But, You made the greatest sacrifice imaginable to stand in the gap for me. Thank You, Jesus. Now, in Your strength empower me to stand in the gap for others. In Your name I pray, Amen."*

## Interruption 1:

If you've made the pledge to stand in the gap, I encourage you to complete your commitment by signing your name to the "standing in the gap" pledge card on page 149.

rock your world

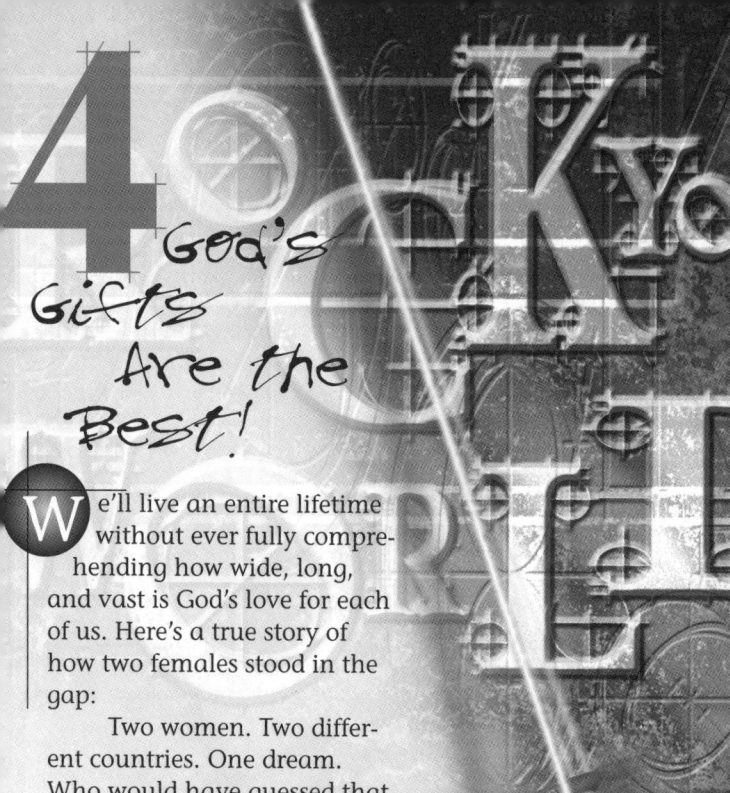

# 4

## God's Gifts Are the Best!

W e'll live an entire lifetime without ever fully comprehending how wide, long, and vast is God's love for each of us. Here's a true story of how two females stood in the gap:

Two women. Two different countries. One dream. Who would have guessed that God would bring them together, across the miles, across two generations, and through one of His creations and their mutual love—a horse.

Rebecca Nielson, a 36-year-old mom living in Gaylord, Michigan, who, along with her husband, owns and operates High Tower Morgan Farms—an immaculate horse ranch in Michigan.

Karen McGregor is a 17-year-old 11th-grader in Calgary, Alberta, who has dreamed of owning a horse since she was three. Everything in her bedroom shows that she isn't just a girl who loves horses—she's a girl who's either part horse or has horse blood running through her veins.

Her room is jam packed with ceramic horses, stuffed horses, and posters of horses. She even has files overflowing with photographs of horses.

*Karen:* A few years ago, I pretended I had a farm, and I cut out pictures of literally hundreds of horses. I gave them all names, created their lineage, and recorded their talents, training, and age in these files. Then I arranged them in sections—stallions at the front of the files, mares with their foals, then geldings.

Hmmm. It would be an understatement to say that Karen loves horses. But the story gets even more interesting. Watch how the lives of Rebecca and Karen begin to intertwine before they even know each other!

## Way Back When

Before Karen was even born, Rebecca was falling in love with horses in Pickford, Michigan.

*Rebecca:* At age three I can remember having four horses and a donkey. I was so in love with the horses, I broke my parent's rules to be with them. And that meant I got spanked every single day. I'd sneak out of the house, grab our dog leash, and head toward the field. I wasn't supposed to be in the field alone because my folks were afraid I'd get hurt, but my love for the horses kept pulling me back (even though I knew it meant a spanking).

I'd hook the dog leash onto one of the horse's halters when he was lying down and sort of pounce on him until he'd get up and let me take him to the field. I established a deep friendship with these animals. It was an unexplainable bond. I could communicate with them. It was like we had our own language.

Meanwhile, at another time, and in another country, three-year-old Karen longed for a horse so desperately that she pretended she was one.

*Karen:* Our family had a trampoline, and I'd jump for hours, pretending I was a horse in training. When that got old, I imagined I was the trainer. I took great care to feed, water, and brush this imaginary horse.

One day I saw a huge, plastic, life-size toy horse in a nearby store. I begged Mom to buy it so we could keep it in the backyard. I couldn't imagine anything better than being able to actually sit on that thing all day long and pretend he was real. But since it cost $1,500, my parents concluded it was a luxury we couldn't afford.

*Rebecca:* When I was older, my parents felt OK about allowing me to ride alone. My horse's name was King, and we did everything together. He was literally my best friend.

We rode all over the place. I'd crawl underneath him, use his neck as a slide, and even slide off his rear end. He threw my sister off, but I was truly his best buddy because if I fell off, he'd stop and wait for me to get up.

When I was in the fourth grade, my dad got transferred, so we sold our horses, left the farm, and moved to another town. It broke my heart to say good-bye to King, but I knew he'd have a good home.

I bought my first horse when I was 15. To do this, I had to work two jobs. I washed dishes at an A&W hamburger stand, then rode my bike five miles to clean a woman's house. She let me buy a horse from her for $400. He had to stay at her place, since we no longer had a barn.

# Dreamin' the Dream

Meanwhile, Rebecca grew up, got married, and fulfilled her love of horses by centering her career on them. Karen, however, still dreamed of someday owning a real horse.

*Karen:* I knew if I was ever going to get a horse, I'd have to work extremely hard and save my money. Dad hired me as his carpenter's assistant, and we began building and renovating our home. He thought my attitude was good, so after a few months of working together, he raised my salary from minimum wage to $6 an hour.

I began to check the prices for various horses. I knew I wouldn't be able to afford much, so I inquired about horses being sent to the glue factory. But even they were going for as much as $1,200 (about $1.50 per pound). I continued checking.

After pooling all my money together from baby-sitting, working with Dad, and other odd jobs, I finally saved $1,500. I had my eye on an old horse that was being kept at a riding stable. She was a pinto (a retired trail horse who used to work on an Indian reservation). She was frequently sick and in lousy health. But I could afford her.

When I approached my folks with the idea of purchasing this old horse, they discouraged me from spending so much money on an animal in such bad shape. It really hurt because that was all I could afford.

I pleaded with my parents, but it didn't do any good. They started adding up additional costs such as boarding, food, trailer, and gasoline. I also needed my driver's license to get to the stables and insurance just to drive. It seemed hopeless.

They kept saying it just wasn't logical, and they tried to interest me in other hobbies and sports. I was so frustrated and hurt. To keep dreaming was incredibly painful. Would it be impossible to get a horse? How could I make them understand that a horse was everything to me?

*Everything?*

Well, owning a horse was very important. Major important. But it really wasn't *everything.* Karen also had a strong relationship with Jesus Christ. She was involved in her church's youth group and consistently prayed about the horse *and* about her walk with God.

Karen has also been a *Brio* Sis (a member of *Brio Magazine* for teen girls) for several years. When she received the 1995 November issue, she was especially drawn to a paragraph announcing a *Brio* mission trip to Bolivia.

*Karen:* I read the announcement and clearly sensed God nudging me to apply. I knew I might not even be selected to participate, but I was keenly aware that He wanted me to apply.

The cost was $1,450 plus my airfare to and from Miami. That meant I would not only have to use all of my horse savings but also need to earn more money in order to cover the rest of the trip.

The more I prayed about it, the more I sensed God leading me to give up my horse money for this mission trip. As soon as I promised to obey Him, I realized I was also giving up my dream of ever owning a horse. It had taken me *so* long to earn $1,500. Realistically, I wouldn't be able to save that much again. It was now or never.

I obeyed God's leading. I applied and was chosen to go to Bolivia in July of 1996. And boy was it a life-changer! We were face-to-face with poverty, visited several Compassion projects, and saw firsthand the difference a sponsorship can make in a child's life. We sang Spanish praise choruses, played with children, held crying babies, and met with *Brio* Sisses who lived in Bolivia as missionary's kids.

Even though I'd been on mission trips before and had done stuff with my youth group, this was completely different. It was incredible to be with a group of *Brio* girls who are my sisters in Christ. I'd never had that kind of deep, intimate, Christian fellowship before.

As the trip continued, God gave me a growing peace that I had done the right thing by obeying Him and giving up my horse money. I wouldn't trade that mission trip for anything in the world!

## God's Dreams Never Die

The girls returned from Bolivia in late July, and the *Brio* staff began putting the story together for the 1996 November issue—exactly one year after Karen had read the announcement.

*Rebecca:* My 16-year-old daughter, Amanda, receives *Brio,* and once in a while I'll sneak a peek at it before she gets home from school.

I was folding laundry when it arrived. My husband, David, brought in the mail and began flipping through the magazine. The story about the Bolivia mission trip caught his eye. He began reading aloud: "Karen had wanted a horse for as long as she could remember, but as soon as she had saved a good amount, she heard the Lord telling her to spend her money instead on a mission trip. So Karen gave up her life-long dream and invested herself and her money in people."

My husband continued reading the story as my eyes filled with tears. Because of my love for God—and my love for horses—I immediately connected with this girl.

I looked up at David and said, "We could make her dream come true. We could give her one of our Morgan horses."

## Across the Miles

Rebecca quickly found the number to Focus on the Family and asked for the *Brio* office. When she reached me, she said, "Susie, you don't know me, but my daughter gets *Brio.* I'm blown away by this girl named Karen who gave up her horse money to go on the Bolivia mission trip.

"I grew up going to Sunday School, church, Vacation Bible School, and even singing in the choir when I was young, but my commitment to God *then* wasn't at all what it is *now*. If God had asked *me* to give up my horse and go on a mission trip, I don't think I would have done it.

"God is speaking to me, Susie. He's saying, 'I can use you to give Karen a powerful miracle—a memory of a lifetime.' I want to be obedient, as Karen was. My husband is in agreement. We want to give Karen a horse and make her dream come true."

*Is it Christmas?*

While Karen was still in school, I phoned her mom. "You're not gonna believe this! But, can Karen have a horse? Rebecca Nielson wants to give her one! All the way from Michigan!"

Karen's mom was speechless but was finally able to ask, "What kind of horse? Karen has dreamed of owning a Morgan horse forever."

"Wow!" I screamed. "It's a miracle. Rebecca raises Morgans! And they sell anywhere from $1,500 to $175,000!"

Karen's folks began talking with Rebecca and making plans for Karen to visit High Tower Morgan Farms.

*Karen:* I couldn't believe it! I still can't believe it! Rebecca invited me to spend a week at her ranch to get to know the horses, ride them, and decide which one I wanted. It was so much fun! Amanda and I cleaned stalls, bleached and washed water buckets, had sawdust fights, fed grain, and mostly rode horses.

When I headed back to Canada at the end of November, I had taken a million photos of a horse I truly fell in love with —Stormy, a beautiful black Morgan.

# The Dream Becomes Reality

**Rebecca:** Although Stormy had already been trained to ride, I wanted him to be at his absolute best by the time I gave him to Karen. So I sent him for further training at a Morgan farm in Ohio, where he learned to walk, trot, and canter—down pat.

Then in April, I drove to Ohio, put him in a long trailer hooked onto the back of my truck, and I drove him to Canada.

Karen: I can still see him coming off the trailer! He proudly galloped and snorted as he pranced all around. It was obvious that he loved people right from the start. He seemed so happy.

Stormy is the best horse in the world! We're genuine friends. I love him! It blows me away that God would direct someone to give me such an incredible gift.

It may sound like this story is all about obeying God, but I don't really look at it that way. If you're thinking I'm some kind of super-Christian who easily sacrificed what I wanted, you're wrong. It was hard. I struggled with giving up my horse money.

The miracle is not that I was obedient. The miracle is that our Heavenly Father loves to give His children wonderful gifts. And not because we deserve them! I certainly don't deserve Stormy.

But what a miracle to realize we serve a God who loves us so much that He enjoys giving us things we don't always need. Because I didn't need a horse—I just desperately wanted one.

## Gifts and Rewards

Hmmm. A Heavenly Father who loves to give good gifts to His children? And think about it, the *best* gift you could ever receive is yours for the asking—eternal life! We can't earn it, and none of us deserve it, but we can have the gift of eternal life simply for the asking.

Karen chose to stand in the gap. She chose to give it all away—not knowing what the future held. As far as she was concerned, she was actually dying to her dream of ever owning a horse.

Rebecca, too, chose to stand in the gap. She gave away one of her beloved horses. But guess what? She now has a lifetime friendship with Karen and her entire family. They visit each other often. And because God knows He can trust her to give away what He's blessed her with—He keeps right on blessing her!

See, the cool thing is that we just can't out give God! He keeps giving, and blessing, and being faithful. *God rewards our obedience.* He doesn't always reward it in this lifetime—sometimes He chooses to wait until we're in heaven to bestow His blessings on us. But He *does* reward our obedience. Never doubt it!

*"God's Gifts Are the Best!" by Susie Shellenberger, originally appeared in the February 1998 edition of* Brio *magazine.*

# 5 Rock Your School

We've already talked about the importance of changing ourselves, and why the world needs changing. Now let's head toward an all-too-familiar place: school.

There are several ways that you can rock your institution of learning. (Translation: *You* can make some positive changes in your school!) One of the most publicized ways to take a stand for Christ is to participate in "See You at the Pole" every September.

"See You at the Pole occurs the third Wednesday of September each year. Call the SYATP Hotline 619-592-9200 for more information."

Though it is *legal* to stand by your school flagpole, it's not always easy. Listen to what Greeley, Colorado, teen Lindy Morgan experienced.

When Lindy took a stand at her flagpole during her freshman year of high school, she met some resistance.

"Buses began pulling in around 7:30 A.M.," Lindy says, "but the students at my school aren't allowed inside the building until the bell rings, so most of the student body was outside while my friends and I were praying at the flagpole.

"One of the school administrators approached me and asked to speak with me. And with a demeaning voice, he said we had to stop. I asked to schedule an appointment with him so that I could bring in materials and my pastor in order to explain that prayer at school *is* constitutional. Not expecting that response from me, he turned the affair over to the principal."

The bell rang, and rumors that Lindy had been "busted" began to fly.

"But I knew God was in control," Lindy says. "At lunch, I was approached by the same administrator, *and he apologized!* Then the principal thanked me for lifting up our school in prayer. Later that day, I was able to witness to a group of girls because of what had happened."

## You Have Rights

You may or may not realize it, but as a student, you're protected by a specific bill of rights. The constitutions of both the United States and Canada protect your freedom of religious expression. For my readers living in the United States, do you know what you *can* and *can't* do on a public school campus? Take this quiz and find out.

Students can pray on a public school campus.

[ ] YES [ ] NO

Students can read their Bibles on a public school campus.

[ ] YES [ ] NO

Students can form religious clubs on campus
if other noncurricular clubs exist.

[ ] YES [ ] NO

Students can hand out tracks, flyers,
or other religious materials on campus.

[ ] YES [ ] NO

Students can do research papers, speeches, etc.,
with religious themes.

[ ] YES [ ] NO

Students can be exempt from participating in assignments
that are contrary to their religious beliefs.

[ ] YES [ ] NO

Students can discuss religious issues although
other students may overhear them.

[ ] YES [ ] NO

Guess what? The answer to all of the above questions is YES! If you'd like to learn more about your religious freedom, get your hands on *Students' Legal Rights on a Public School Campus* ($10). To request a copy, write: See You at the Pole, P.O. Box 60134, Fort Worth, TX 76115. Or call 1-817-HIS-PLAN.

Right now let's take a quick peek at the rights you legally have as a student.

# Students' Bill of Rights on a Public School Campus

**1.** *THE RIGHT to meet with other religious students.* The Equal Access Act allows students the freedom to meet on campus for the purpose of discussing religious issues.

**2.** *THE RIGHT to identify your religious beliefs through signs and symbols.* Students are free to express their religious beliefs through signs and symbols.

**3.** *THE RIGHT to talk about your religious beliefs on campus.* Freedom of speech is a fundamental right mandated in the Constitution and does not exclude the schoolyard.

**4.** *THE RIGHT to distribute religious literature on campus.* Distributing literature on campus may not be restricted simply because it is religious.

**5.** *THE RIGHT to pray on campus.* Students may pray alone or with others so long as it does not disrupt school activities or is not forced on others.

**6.** *THE RIGHT to carry or study your Bible on campus.* The Supreme Court has said that only *state directed* Bible reading is unconstitutional. Students may bring their Bibles to school.

**7.** *THE RIGHT to do research papers, speeches, and creative projects with religious themes.* The First Amendment to the Constitution does not forbid all mention of religion in public schools.

**8.** *THE RIGHT to be exempt.* Students may be exempt from activities and class content that contradict their religious beliefs.

**9.** *THE RIGHT to celebrate or study religious holidays on campus.* Music, art, literature, and drama that have religious themes are permitted as part of the curriculum for school activities if presented in an objective manner as a traditional part of the cultural and religious heritage of the particular holiday.

**10.** *THE RIGHT to meet with school officials.* The First Amendment forbids Congress to make any law that would restrict the right of the people to petition the Government (school officials).

*(This information applies primarily to United State's students and was excerpted with permission from* Students' Legal Rights *by J. W. Brinkley with K. C. Crump, © 1993, Roever Communications.)*

Teens all over the world are taking strong stands for Jesus Christ. It's not always easy, but it *is* always rewarding. Here's a true story about three guys who dared to be vocal.

# On Fire in Florida

## by Michael Ross

"Hey, Bible Boy. Where's your Word?" shouts a voice from across the crowded hall.

Fifteen-year-old Eric Stueberg grins and holds up a tattered book with fluorescent lime green words—HOLY BIBLE—handwritten across the cover.

"Right here," he says. "Wouldn't leave home without it!"

It's Monday morning at Florida's Fort Walton Beach High School, and Eric loves his new reputation. When other guys return from the weekend bragging about how far they've gone with a girl or how much they had to drink, Eric can't stop boasting about his radical God—and how far Christ can take a life that's fired-up for Him.

It all started a few months back when Eric and some of his church friends realized they had work to do for God—starting with their own lives.

"During one of our revival services at our church, the Lord came and His Spirit poured out on our church. It was amazing," Eric says. "And when the pastor invited people to the altar, my friends and I knew we needed to go forward."

The message from Revelation 3:15—about being lukewarm— had touched a nerve. Eric realized that he wasn't on track with Jesus, and that attending church on Sundays and Wednesdays wasn't enough.

"You have to *know* Jesus," Eric says. "He has to be your best friend—your Lord.

"I thought about how half my school wasn't saved," Eric continues. "I knew I needed to make a change in my life, then reach out to other teens. I finally stood up and went down to the altar. Everything just broke. It was a real turnaround."

One of the first things Eric and his friend Jill Broxson did was start a Bible study at school. The second—and most important, he says—was to step out as a "walking billboard."

"Some teens wear Christian T-shirts and go to church, but they also spend their weekends partying," Eric says. "I used to be that way too. But I've seen how it can completely ruin a Christian's witness."

Today, he's convinced that if you're claiming to be Christian, you'd better live like it. After all, being a walking billboard means people will read your life. "I want people to read 'JESUS' when they see me," he says. "That's why I love being called Bible Boy. It's cool."

But being radical for God comes at a cost. Eric lost a few friends who thought he'd become too religious, and he occasionally gets picked on. "Let's not kid ourselves; taking a stand for God is far from easy," Eric says. "But who says following Jesus should be easy?"

The first few weeks were the hardest. But, gradually, casual friends began calling him Bible Boy—with a positive tone—and some even visited his campus Bible study. And what began as a handful of teens who would spend their lunch hour praying, now fills a room.

"This world needs bold Christians," Eric says, "especially teenagers who are willing to stand in the face of what's popular and say, 'Jesus is the ONLY truth, the ONLY life, and the ONLY way.'

"As far as being rejected, I don't want to stand before God on Judgment Day and hear the words, 'I counted on you to tell your friends about Me, but you didn't.'

"I don't want my friends to spend eternity in hell. I can't be selfish. I've got to speak up and do my part to rock my school for Christ."

And Eric's commitment is making a difference. "Today, I'm not the only 'Bible Boy' at school," he says. "There are a lot of us now. And that's awesome."

# How to Start a Christian Club

Fifteen-year-old Eric Stueberg took a bold step by starting a campus Bible study group—and YOU can too!

But remember: The purpose of starting a Christian club isn't to create a "holy huddle" or a special clique, but to be a light where God has placed you—and to love and serve your campus for Christ.

As Eric discovered, not every student will want to join. But as you begin to meet needs on your campus, some will want to know more about the One who loves them most—and who can meet the deepest need of their heart.

## Here's how to get started:

1. PRAY with friends.
2. Pick a NAME.
3. Select a SPONSOR.
4. Choose an ENCOURAGER.
5. Prepare a CONSTITUTION.
6. Present a PROPOSAL to your principal.
7. PUBLICIZE your new club.
8. Pick up a copy of *The Christian Club Guide* ($1.95).

This resource will explain each of the above steps. To request this resource, write: See You at the Pole, P.O. Box 60134, Fort Worth, TX 76115. Or call 1-817-HIS-PLAN.

*"On Fire in Florida" first appeared in the November 1997 issue of* Breakaway *magazine.*

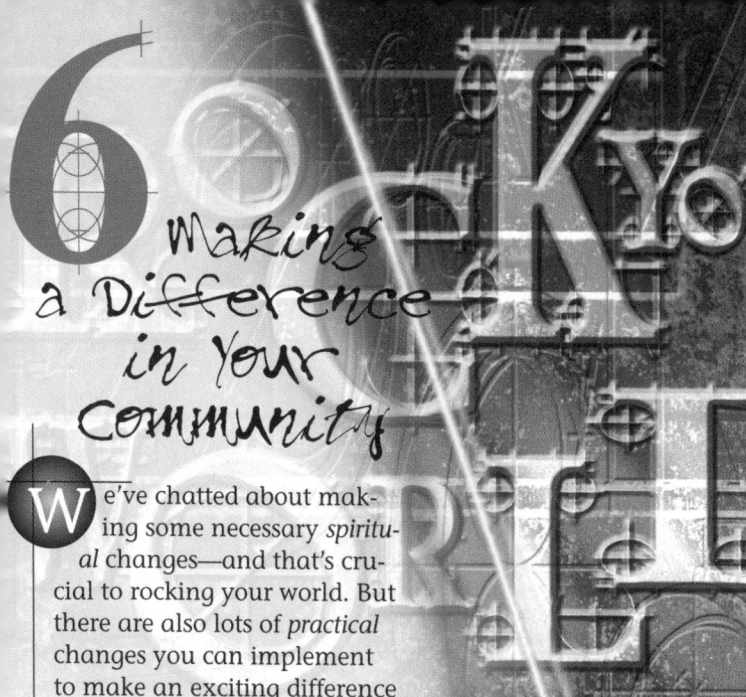

# 6
## Making a Difference in Your Community

### Your World

W e've chatted about making some necessary *spiritual* changes—and that's crucial to rocking your world. But there are also lots of *practical* changes you can implement to make an exciting difference in your world. Let's start with what you can do right where you are, OK? Meet some young men and women your age who are taking the dare to change their world!

"I made a difference at my school and church when my class of 20 teens planted 400 white crosses in front of the church. Each cross represented 10 aborted babies in the United States. This was our way of taking a stand against abortion.

"We were criticized for this display because not everyone believes that abortion is wrong. We had *so* many responses, and they varied from those who were extremely angry with us to others who referred to us as 'angels.'

"Planting 400 white crosses on a main city highway really showed our love for life and our faithfulness to our majestic Lord!"

—*Alecia Pennington,*
*Geneva, Illinois.*

"Every day during my senior year of high school I got out a half day early, because I visited people in a nursing home. The more I went, the more I began to realize that these were people just like me—only older. They had some of the same needs I did. They wanted to be loved, they got lonely, they enjoyed talking, and they wanted to know that they mattered."

—*Jonathan Pierce*
*contemporary Christian artist*

A group of teens in Bremerton, Washington are not only proud of their sexual purity, they're encouraging others to hop on the wagon of abstinence. This group of Christian teens calls themselves BAVAM! (Born Again Virgins of America!) They believe that meeting together regularly encourages accountability for the promises they've each made to themselves and to God. There are currently more chapters being formed across the United States and Canada.

"I was known in high school as the 'Dr. Pepper man' because I didn't drink alcohol. I didn't come across as preachy or judgmental; I just let my actions speak for themselves. Even though that was a few years ago, I often receive letters or phone calls from people I went to high school with who say, 'You know, that really meant a lot that you didn't drink.' And 'You didn't know it then, but your stand against drinking really made me think.' You never know how your very lifestyle can influence those around you."

—*Jonathan Pierce*

"My brother Stephen and I have been running a children's Bible club for a few years in the village where we live. It's aimed at children ages 4 to 12 years, and we hold it once a week in the local community center.

"Each week we sing lots of songs about Jesus, we talk about the importance of loving God, and we witness. We also have a Bible lesson, a memory verse, a quiz, and lots of fun games that the kids love.

"Before the Bible club starts, we always have a short prayer meeting where we discuss the club and specific prayer requests. Then we pray for each other, the kids in the Bible club, and ask God to use us to spread the gospel to the children who come.

"I really enjoy it, and I love working with kids. It's so rewarding! On the last night of the Bible club—before it stopped for the summer holidays—a little six-year-old girl told us that she became a Christian! It's great to know that these children are receiving and accepting the good news of Jesus Christ! That's the absolute best feeling in the world!"

—*Susan Renton,*
*Wemyss Bay, Scotland*

There's More!

Still looking for some creative ways to make a difference in the community you live in? Try these simple suggestions:

# World's Largest Piggy Bank.

Everyone has a little loose change—even teens! Why not take advantage of it? Designate a bucket in your house, several of your friend's houses, in your youth group, your classes at school, and in your community center. Ask everyone to drop their loose change in the buckets. Imagine! If we all worked together and gave a few cents every day, we could make a giant difference.

Make sure everyone understands that you're not asking for checks or paper money. You're concentrating simply on loose change—a few cents from everyone who can afford to get rid of some extra coins.

Decide ahead of time how often you'll collect the buckets (once a month, once every two months). Combine all the buckets together in a gigantic box or container, and designate that as your "World's Largest Piggy Bank."

You'll also want to decide ahead of time where you'll donate the money. Get some help making this decision. Ask your pastor, your city leaders, and your parents for their suggestions. There may be a local college that needs scholarship funds for students lacking money for tuition. Or you might know of a children's hospital, a halfway house, or some other area of need.

Announce the results after three months, and send the information to your local paper. Ordinary people doing extra things to help others is the best kind of news to report—and to read! Not only will this inform your community of what's going on, but hopefully, it will inspire others to give their loose change to the "World's Largest Piggy Bank."

# Earth Facts

## by Susan M. Stevens

*Take this three-step plan to saving the planet!*

Are you concerned about the Earth and the way it's being damaged—even destroyed—by our pollution? Wanna take some solid steps that'll help mend the mistakes?

Yes?! Great! Read on . . . because this simple "Three-Step Plan to Saving the Planet" includes a ton of cool stuff you can do.

## Step 1: Get Involved

- Consider starting a club in your school that's geared to improving the environment. If one already exists, join it and help keep it active and exciting!
- Get your youth group to participate in the Adopt-a-Highway litter control program.
- Involve your parents and see what you can do as a family.

## Step 2: Think Environmentally

Before you toss that aluminum can or step into your usual shower-by-the-hour routine, stop and ask yourself a few questions: "Can I recycle this piece of trash?" "Am I being wasteful during my daily routines?"

Some conservation-minded things you can do are as simple as using a lower-wattage bulb in your lamps—and even shutting them off when you leave the room. Here are some more helpful hints:

*Tips for Saving the Tap*

- Take a shorter shower. A five-minute shower uses less water than a bath.
- Turn off the water while brushing your teeth, soaping your face or scrubbing dishes.
- Keep a jug of water in the fridge rather than running the faucet until it gets cold.
- Collect water in containers while letting the shower or faucet warm up, then use it later to water plants.
- Only run washing machines or dishwashers with full loads.
- Sweep sidewalks rather than hosing them off.
- Water your lawn during the coolest part of the day to avoid major evaporation.
- Wash Dad's car with a bucket of soapy water, using the hose only to rinse off the car when finished.
- If you see a leak, tell your parents immediately. Even a tiny leak can waste several dollars of water a day.

*Tips for Making the Extra Effort*

- Walk or ride your bike whenever possible—you can enjoy more of God's creation, and the exercise is *great!*
- Take the train or bus for longer trips.

- Do all your errands in one car trip.

- Carpool to youth group meetings and other activities that aren't accessible by public transportation.

- Keep the heat turned down in your house and wear more layers of clothing.

- Turn off lights and appliances that aren't being used.

- Use closed curtains to block heat in summer; open them to let heat in during the winter.

- Use natural light whenever possible (but don't damage your eyes by not using enough).

- Put a blanket at the bottom of drafty doors and windows.

- Close doors to closets and rooms not being used to save heat and air-conditioning energy (and cost).

## Tips for Managing Your Mealtime

- Prepare only what you'll eat.

- Eat more veggies—they're easier for the food chain to produce than meat and are a better use of resources.

- Plant a garden—you'll get great satisfaction from eating your own produce.

- After wintertime baking, turn the oven off and open its door to warm up the kitchen.

- Cover pots on the stove when cooking to help them heat faster.

- Use your dinner plate for dessert as well—you'll save water, energy and elbow grease by washing fewer dishes.

- Talk with your mom about using cloth napkins, which can be used for a few meals and then washed, rather than paper napkins, which are thrown into the trash after each meal.

- Plan ahead before you get into your fridge—try to get out everything you need at one time, keeping more cold air in.

## Step 3: Know the Facts

You've probably heard this saying from your parents: "The more you know, the further you'll go." It's true! And the more you understand about conservation, the more steps you can take to protect our planet. Fill your noggin with these nature facts:

- Americans recycle about 56 percent of the 200 million aluminum cans purchased *daily*.
- The cans thrown away each year by America would wrap around the earth's equator 164 times.
- The average American uses an estimated 639 pounds of paper annually (eight times the world average), and recycles about 25 percent of that.
- Disposable diapers cost an average of $1,716 per child. Cloth diapers washed in the home cost an average of $975 per child during the same amount of time.

*"Earth Facts" by Susan Stevens first appeared in the 1993 April issue of Brio magazine.*

## Interruption 2

**Look on page 151 for what two teen girls did for their community.**

Still looking for something to do? Check out this true story of how one teen girl helped hundreds of underprivileged families!

# Christmas Angels

## by Maria Fasal Faulconer

Fifteen-year-old Heather Sharkey sat curled up on the sofa in the living room of her Colorado Springs home holding a miniature angel by its slender gold thread. "We gave one of these gifts to each of our friends to thank them for being our Christmas angels," she said.

Two weeks earlier, Heather and her mom had given a Christmas Angel Tea and more than 130 moms and daughters came! What made it so special was the fact that everyone brought a gift for a needy family.

"Before Thanksgiving," Heather said, "Mom and I were talking about the holidays and how sad it must be for families struggling to make ends meet. We had this wild idea to combine entertaining with helping."

They sent out an invitation trimmed in holly and red ribbons:

*In the spirit of the coming*
*Holiday Season*
*Please come to a*
*Christmas Angel Tea*
*Sunday, December 15*
*1-4 P.M.*
*and bring a gift or*
*a food basket.*

# A Dream Fulfilled

For Heather, the tea was the fulfillment of a dream she'd had since returning from a church-sponsored mission trip to Tijuana, Mexico, two years earlier. "One of our jobs in Mexico was to give baths to children from a local orphanage. We put them in metal tubs filled with hot water and de-liced them," she said. "If enough clothes had been donated that month, we threw away their old ones. If there weren't enough, we put the same filthy clothes back on the children. What amazed me was how grateful they were for even a T-shirt. They had nothing, and yet they were so happy. We have everything, and it never seems to be enough.

"There wasn't any electricity where we stayed. We slept on concrete floors, and every time we used the outhouse, the door was so shaky that we were afraid it would fall on top of us. But it was the neatest experience of my life, because it opened my eyes to the world around me. It made me realize that I'm part of something greater than myself—that we're all brothers and sisters in Christ.

"Ever since that trip," she says, "I've wanted to help out in my community. The tea was the perfect idea!"

# Making Plans

What began with a vision, snowballed beyond the Sharkey's wildest dreams. From the very beginning, everyone wanted to help. "We needed to find a place big enough to hold the tea," Heather remembers. "So we called a school that had several large meeting rooms. When we explained what we were doing and why, the principal simply donated the space to us!

"Since it was a mother/daughter tea, we decided to help single moms who were struggling to raise families on their own. We called the Ecumenical Social Ministries—a Christian nonprofit organization—and found out they had an adopt-a-family program."

After receiving a list of families, Heather and her mom started calling their friends. "The phone didn't stop ringing for a month!" Heather recalls. "It was so fun to talk to friends I hadn't heard from in a long time."

Heather and her mom didn't mind spending hours on the phone, because they wanted their friends to know each needy family's situation and every child's name.

"I took so much for granted," Heather says. "One mom, who worked as a maid in a hotel, couldn't even afford bed frames. Her kids slept on mattresses on the floor. Another mom was a widow. Even though all she could find were temporary jobs, she made it without food stamps—even with four teenagers!"

One little boy's dream was to own a skateboard. Since it was so expensive, Heather and her mom called North Shore, a local company, hoping for a discount. They were amazed when North Shored donated their top of the line model and the manufacturer replaced the store's skateboard free of charge.

Friends offered to bring cookies, brownies, and platters of cheese and crackers. Restaurants and catering companies donated food. "Mom and I bought small artificial Christmas trees for each family, and friends volunteered to provide the decorations."

Right before the tea, Heather realized she didn't have any table decorations. "Mom happened to talk with a friend who said she'd been collecting angels for years and gladly volunteered them. Then this woman mentioned that the Ecumenical Social Ministries had helped *her* several years before. She was thrilled to give something back."

The Spirit of Jesus was at work!

# The Day Arrives

The day before the tea, Heather had another idea. "We wanted to thank everyone for their help, so we bought 150 miniature plastic angels (we got them at a great discount) and stayed up until 2 A.M. spray-painting them with gold glitter. Then we attached them to a list of acknowledgments."

Temperatures barely rose above zero the day of the tea, but nothing could dampen the spirits of the moms and daughters who streamed into the school with armloads of gifts and platters of food. As younger sisters ran from table to table stacking them high with gifts, one mom had tears in her eyes. "This is what Christmas is all about!" she said.

After the tea, the gifts and food baskets were taken to a downtown church for distribution later in the week. Heather helped with the work after school. "I was so moved," she says. "One mom hugged me and said, 'This is an answer to prayer for me and my family.'

"I couldn't help but think of Isaiah 40:31," Heather says. "'But those who hope in the Lord will renew their strength. They will soar on wings like eagles; they will run and not grow weary, they will walk and not be faint.'"

As the director of the adopt-a-family program watched the families pick up their gifts, she shook her head. "Heather and her mom are incredible," she said. "It's overwhelming to see the impact their efforts have had in the community. They have collected more than 150 gifts!"

All it took was a dream and two special angels.

# 7

## Keep Rocking!

There are still *more* ways that you can rock your world and make a difference. Have you ever considered sponsoring a child? Several Christian organizations offer this ministry.

I've been overseas with Compassion International and have seen firsthand what their organization is all about. Their program revolves around sponsors who donate $28 a month to help meet the needs of an underprivileged child.

## But What IS Sponsorship?

When someone agrees to sponsor a child, it doesn't mean he's adopted someone or that the child is going to show up on his doorstep. It *does* mean that by giving $28 a month, you're providing a needy child with schooling (at a church-sponsored school), clothing, a hot meal every day, school supplies, and best of all, discipleship. With education, skills, and a relationship with Christ, many children have the opportunity to either leave the poverty they were born in, or stay close to their village and raise the standard of living for their families—all because of the knowledge and skills gained through being a sponsored child.

## It Really DOES Make a Difference!

One of the Compassion projects (term for a church-sponsored school) that I visited overseas was teaching students all the expected subjects (math, science, etc.) But they had also gone a step further and were teaching the children how to plant and grow vegetables, the importance of cleanliness, and fundamental skills in music and sports. The children will then be able to raise the quality of life for their families because of what they learn in the project.

In amazement I watched as children played violins, sang in choirs, tilled the garden, played soccer, and responded to the teacher's questions over a variety of subjects. If these children hadn't been sponsored, chances are they would have never even *heard* a violin or choir. Sponsorship makes all the difference in the world.

*Yeah, but $28 a month is a lot of money!* Well, that's kind of true. But remember, we're talking about standing in the gap. Making a difference. Rocking your world. That requires sacrifice. Remember, making a difference will cost. It won't always be easy, but it *will* always be right!

When you think about it, $28 a month really boils down to a couple of pizzas. Think you could give up pizza twice a month to change someone's life?

## "$28 equals a couple of pizzas"

Hmmm. Certainly worth considering, don't you think?

### Let's take a trip

Every time we see a special on an endangered species or an animal (like the white-furred seal) being bludgeoned for its fur, we're outraged. People respond with immediate action.

Yet right now, something far more horrendous happens every day and goes almost unnoticed. Thirty-five thousand children die, and hardly anyone hears their whimpers. *Thirty-five thousand children a day!* Hard to imagine, isn't it? Hard for *me* too. That's why I called Compassion International and started asking questions. They, in turn, asked me to accompany them to Brazil so I could see firsthand what their ministry is all about. Step inside my scrapbook and let me show you around, OK?

### You work where?

One of our priority stops was the dump. This isn't like one of *our* garbage dumps. *This* dump goes for *miles!* All the city's garbage is dumped here several times a day.

People actually live and work here. Kids as young as three years old (and on up through adulthood) work from 7 A.M. to 7 P.M., then they begin again at 10 P.M. and work until 3 A.M. They're constantly foraging through all the garbage for stuff they can sell. There are three basic items: cans, aluminum, and paper. Then, recycling companies arrive and pay them anywhere from $1 to $3 for their loot.

You could make more than that just baby-sitting for a couple of hours. Kind of makes you want to count your blessings, doesn't it?

It's a *dump,* so you can imagine the extreme filth. But what you *can't* imagine is the sordid stench. Most of the people wear rags (even though they're dirty) around their faces to help shield the smell.

This has to be one of the worst jobs imaginable. The dump is a rat-infested, vulture-filled trap. The people describe it as "hell."

It's also extremely dangerous. Only a week before I arrived, a child fell off the top of a truck and was killed. And because there are no restrictions on what can and can't be taken to the dump, it's like walking through a mine field of dirty hypodermic needles, toxic waste, and chemical acids—many times *barefooted!*

## The Boy From the Dump

But now let me show you a glimpse of hope. Meet Zeka. He was discovered by accident. Five years ago, the Compassion film crew was getting shots of life in the dump for a television special. They noticed a 12-year-old boy with a dirty rag around his foot. So they zoomed the camera in on him and started asking questions.

Zeka explained (through an interpreter—because all of Brazil speaks Portuguese) that he'd stepped on a nail, and it had gone right through his foot. Someone had removed it, and although it was wrapped, it was extremely infected.

The film crew took him to the hospital, got his foot treated, and brought his picture back to America in hopes that *someone* would sponsor him. Someone did.

But, guess what? There's more!

Zeka now goes to school and is being trained as a teacher's aide. He gets paid the same amount he was making before in the dump. His mom still works the dump, but because *just one person* dared to share $28 a month with Zeka, his entire life has turned right side up. He and his mom have both accepted Jesus Christ as their personal Savior.

## Alena's Agony

Now let me introduce you to Alena. She's 13 years old and has been working the dump for only a few months. She has nothing to smile about. Life is only a matter of survival.

I asked her what she did for fun. Alena simply stared at me with blank eyes and finally said, "I don't have fun."

She'll keep working the dump, keep living in poverty, and have no hope and no future—unless *someone* decides to shell out $28 a month.

**MAJOR INSPIRATION!** *You* (or you and your youth group) could take Alena out of the dump! You could make a lifetime difference for Alena. And for many more just like her.

I only visited one section of the dump, and there were probably a thousand people working that specific area. It goes on and on for miles. We know it's tough enough to work hard on a full stomach, but these people are *starving*. Yet they keep working while feeling dizzy and sick from the stench.

After our visit to the dump, some of the members of our group gave our interpreter some money and asked him to give it to a local church to spend on feeding the people. They did. Know how much it cost? Only nine dollars. Nine dollars bought bread and butter for 1,000 people!

Follow me to the streets. There are 12 million homeless children roaming the streets of Brazil, and it's estimated that 500,000 of them are teenage prostitutes.

They're on the streets for a variety of reasons. First, their family is too poor to care for them, so they're tossed out the door to fend for themselves. Or they're being so severely abused at home that life on the streets seems like a better option.

But it's not really *life* on the streets. It's more like a slow death. These children are *starving.* They're no longer *children* but have become scar-faced, disease-ridden animals. They forage through the garbage for food, steal bread from street merchants, and sell their bodies. They'll do *anything* to eat. It's just a matter of survival.

They're so hungry they often sniff shoe glue to make their stomachs feel full. And then, of course, they're stoned and do dangerous things.

I saw kids run out in the middle of traffic doing cartwheels. Cars darted and swerved. But no one cares if they're hit or run over, because they're *nobody's* kids.

You might think the police would help. But the merchants hate these kids so much (because they steal food) that they bribe the policemen to kill the children. In fact, just last year, "moonlighting" policemen killed almost 5,000 children in Brazil.

Since there are *12 million* children on the streets, it makes it kind of hard to hide. But I *did* find out that when kids learn the police are after them, they'll go underground and hide in the sewer system for *months,* coming out only at night to look for food.

## The Girl from the Streets

There's someone else I want you to meet. Nubia. She's 11 years old. She has absolutely *nothing* to be happy about. She's been on the street for years and will sleep with anyone just for food money. Nubia's never been to school, never known the security of a family who loves her, and above all else, she never had a chance.

After we gave her a bowl of food, we left. Then she went back to the streets.

The most we could do was tell her we loved her and wish her luck, knowing she was going back to having sex with anyone and everyone just to survive.

I didn't sleep much that night. I couldn't get Nubia out of my mind. There's no hope for her. Chances are high that she'll be dead within a year.

The ending to this story *could* change, though. Someone *could* choose to sponsor Nubia and take her off the streets. And love her. And change her life.

The question: *Will someone?*

The answer: I don't know.

The challenge: **Will YOU?**

## So You Wanna Make a Difference?

I hope you won't just read this chapter then toss it aside or hurry through the rest of the book. I'm praying as I write this that you'll allow God to help you *respond* and *act*.

Before I end this chapter, there is one more person I want you to meet: His name is Zezinho. (I call him Z-Boy.) He's my sponsored child. I wouldn't feel right encouraging you to do something that I don't do myself. I know first-hand the lifetime difference sponsorship can make. That's why I'm sponsoring Z-Boy.

When you sponsor someone, you'll receive a card with your child's photo and all kinds of information on it.

You'll also get to write to your child. Your sponsoring organization will send your letter to a translator for rewriting in the child's language, but your child will receive *both* letters.

Every few months you'll receive a letter from your sponsored child (his original letter, plus the translation), and every other year you'll get a progress report (which includes an updated photo and a list of any changes that have occurred in his family: deaths, divorce, births, etc.)

Again, we're talking about sacrificing a couple of pizzas a month to change someone's life. Hmmm. Still thinking about it? How about *acting* on it?

Call or write for more information, OK?

**Compassion International**
**Colorado Springs, CO 80997**
**1-800-336-7676**
**http://www.compassion.com**

# 8 Get Outta Dodge!

**ROCK Your WORLD**

**B**y now you've realized that you can make an incredibly enormous difference in your world by never even leaving your hometown. But sometimes when we actually get involved in rocking our world, it gets so exciting that we want to expand and rock the world in a bigger way by reaching out in an even bigger sense.

Have you ever considered going on a mission trip? I've been on several. And I've talked to lots of teens and adults who have participated in mission trips. Though the stories are different, one thing remains the same: Everyone agrees that a mission trip can change your life!

Let's eavesdrop on a few teens who are talking about *their* experiences with mission trips.

I went on an awesome mission trip to Mexico over Christmas break. We couldn't have accomplished any more than we did. God worked in ways we never even thought of.

I was directly involved in what I believe was the casting out of demonic spirits. We were at a dump ground where people lived, and we showed an evangelistic video in Spanish, performed skits, and gave away a lot of stuff. After the video, we had an altar call, so that the ones who wanted to become Christians could come forward and make a spiritual commitment.

This one teen gave his life to Christ, and then went into a big physical . . . thing. Those around him thought maybe it was a heart attack, but when they checked his pulse it was normal. As far as they could tell, he was OK—but we knew he was definitely *not* OK! We all gathered around him, laid hands on him, and prayed. He kept saying someone or something was there and was keeping him from being OK.

He finally said he trusted Jesus and wouldn't let Satan control him. *That* was when things began to settle down. A great calm came over him. I'd never seen anything like that before—let alone been a part of it!

Another awesome thing that happened to us was on the way home to North Dakota. There were 20-some students on the trip with us who weren't Christians. We had really been praying for them, but it hadn't seemed to do any good.

On the way home, we had bus troubles. That held us up for an entire day. While we were sitting around waiting for the bus to be fixed, I had an incredible talk with one of the girls that wasn't a Christian.

I specifically asked her about her salvation. She didn't respond to what we talked about, but I could tell she was thinking and that God was working.

The next day, as we thought we were parting, we said our good-byes and got on our appropriate buses. But a blizzard hit halfway home, and we had to stay at a church in South Dakota.

Before we left the next morning, we held a service in which different people got up and spoke about their desire to see everyone on the trip saved. It was totally Spirit-led. At the end, more than 20 people decided to let God rule their lives—including the girl I had talked with the night before. It was so cool!

The entire mission trip was absolutely packed with amazing things. The main lesson I learned, though, is that God always works—it's just in His own time. And even when He seems to be taking a long time, He's still at work. Our responsibility is not to understand His timing but to simply trust and continue praying.

—Nathan Opdahl
Grand Forks, North Dakota

Last October, God gave me the opportunity to go on a short-term mission trip to Toyatti, Russia. At 15 years of age, I was only one of two teens on the trip and one of the youngest ever to go on a mission trip from my church.

When I went to the informational meeting, I really didn't think I'd actually end up going. But we watched a video about mission trips, and when I heard a child saying in Russian that he had accepted Christ into his heart, I started crying. I felt an unfamiliar tug on my heart, and during the next few days, I sensed that God was calling me to be a part of this trip.

The leader told me I'd have to have one of my parents accompany me, and we'd need to raise $5,300 to cover expenses for both of us. I talked it over with my parents and we put the possibility in God's hands.

We also sent out 300 support letters to close friends, family, and acquaintances. And guess what? Within two weeks we had the entire $5,300! But that's not all! The letters kept rolling in, and we ended up with an extra $2,000!

As the trip drew nearer, Satan kept tempting our family. *Was this really what we were supposed to be doing?* During this time we learned to trust God even more.

I was pretty jazzed by the time we actually left on the trip. I was prayed up and could feel God's hand directing everything. After a 12-hour flight and a 22-hour train ride, we arrived in Toyatti.

The days that followed were the best days of my life! I gained a much bigger understanding of how incredibly awesome God truly is.

When we arrived in our village we saw a teacher and her students, so we asked where the school was. She led us to the school and invited us to speak to her English class. We spoke for three hours to her students—every day that week—and told them why we were there. We also told them all about Jesus.

Every night at our group meetings 100 children attended. We taught them parables that explained God's never ending love.

On Thursday evening I was given the opportunity to speak, so I talked about the second chapter of Mark and how God can heal you spiritually—how He can make us walk again beside Him in the kingdom of heaven. But like the Pharisees of the law, Satan will try to trap us. In the end, however, God triumphs in victory!

Afterward, I asked if anyone would like to receive Christ as his personal savior. Forty-two children and six adults came forward. I was amazed at how God chose to use my humble efforts.

The next day I had to say good-bye to my new Christian friends. The fact that we will someday spend eternity together, though, made it a little easier to leave.

After I got back from the trip, I had several opportunities to speak to the church and other organizations in town. God opened so many doors I never would have thought possible.

I learned some important things from this experience: To trust in God, no matter what happens, and to take pride in our Lord and Savior. He wants us to be bold with our faith. After all, we're never too young to do the Lord's work.

—*Brian Haley*
*Corinth, Texas*

Hi! I've been on five mission trips with a group called Kings Kids with YWAM (Youth With a Mission).

One summer, we went to Richmond, Virginia. We were performing on the lawn of a recreation center in an area that wasn't too friendly to Christians. As we began our presentation, we heard gunshots from the nonbelievers trying to scare us into leaving.

I was scared! We divided into prayer groups for the next hour and prayed for the shooters and for the people of the town to be more open to Christ. Amazingly, we were able to pray with some of the townspeople and led some into a personal relationship with the Lord.

Although the entire ordeal was frightening, I was reminded in a powerful way that God can work through any situation to accomplish His purpose.

—Candace Chung
Seoul, Korea

Every year our youth group goes on a mission trip to a small town in Mexico. Once we're there, we set up camp just outside of town, and for the next four days we diligently work to build a house for an underprivileged family. This is not only a great time to share the gospel with someone who has probably never heard it before but also a terrific time to evaluate my relationship with God.

I first signed up to go on our youth group's mission trip because all my friends were going, and because I knew we'd be making a stop at Disneyland on our way home.

For the next several weeks, I worked hard to raise the money I needed for the trip. I finally earned the necessary amount and was on my way. But there was still the problem of my motives.

I wanted to hang out in Southern California. What's weird, is the fact that I didn't even realize my priorities were messed up until one Sunday when my mom heard me talking about how excited I was to be going to Disneyland. Mom looked me in the eye and asked me why I was really going on the trip. I couldn't say anything. It hit me. And it hit me hard. My motives were all messed up. I was going for all the wrong reasons. But I wanted to go so bad. So I just stuffed that nagging feeling that something wasn't right deep inside and carried on.

Three weeks later, I boarded a plane for San Diego, California. That night we picked up our rental vans and drove north to Fullerton, California, where we stayed in the dorms at Pacific Christian College.

The following day, we went sightseeing and hung out at Huntington Beach. It was a blast, but I kept thinking about the day we'd be spending in Disneyland later that week.

Early the next morning, we loaded the van and headed toward the border. A few hours later, we pulled into a campground in a little town outside of Tijuana. Tecate was our home for the next four days.

The drive to our work site the next day was one of the most eye-opening experiences I've ever had. I saw a hillside covered with tiny shacks that looked like they were made of cardboard. I noticed children playing among the trash because they had nowhere else to play. That's when my heart began to change—dramatically.

We pulled up to the work site and met the family for whom we'd be building the house. All seven of them lived in a tiny 200-square-foot area. I wouldn't even really call it a house—but it was all they had.

When I learned this, I got down on my knees and asked God to forgive me for how selfish I had been. I thought about how much trouble I gave my parents when I had to share a room with my brother. Man! Our room was about the size of these people's entire home! It was then I realized how much I take for granted. I have the privilege of going to school, getting a solid education, living in a nice home, and getting to grow up in a God-fearing family.

From that moment on, all of my motives for being on the mission trip began to change. I no longer cared that we were going to Disneyland. It didn't matter that it was 115 degrees outside. All I focused on was serving God to the best of my ability. I wanted to do as much as I could to change the lives of those people.

Every night after we were done with our work, we'd light a campfire and have a praise and worship time. This was probably my favorite time of the whole trip. It was awesome to sit around the fire and hear not only the voices of teens in our group but also the hundreds of voices of another language praising our same Jesus. I poured out my heart to God, and He began doing a mighty work in me.

When I returned home, I was again reminded about how blessed I am to be where I am. And when I look back on the trip, I realize I grew immensely in my walk with God. I came back with a whole new outlook on life.

I definitely recommend to anyone who has never been on a mission trip to consider going on one. You really feel great about having a chance to make a difference in someone's life. You'll learn a lot about yourself and God.

I've never seen anyone come back from a trip like ours and not be totally on fire for God. You come back with an intense spiritual focus. You want to do everything you can to be all God wants you to be. Nothing can stop you!

—*Matt Nystrom*
*Marysville, Washington*

I spent three months living in the Ukraine as a missionary just a few months ago. The entire experience was great, and I don't regret a thing about staying there.

My brother and I were working with a mission team called Christ Is the Answer. This was a group of 40 that traveled to different cities in the Ukraine with the gospel. We set up a large tent in every town we visited. We had truck trailers to hold our living needs—like a kitchen, bunks, toilets, an office, etc.

Living in the Ukraine was a lot different than living in Canada. It's like the country is 50 years behind us. The roads, facilities, and houses are all really old and worn down.

And the food was *really* different. A couple of favorites among the people there are borscht, a type of soup, and lots of different fruit. Kvause is a really weird drink made from black bread. Have you ever had plum perogies? They were pretty good, actually! One thing I just couldn't make myself try was the chicken feet soup. (I'm serious!)

I met so many new people and did a lot of new things. Every day we were on the streets singing, sharing testimonies, handing out gospel literature, and visiting hospitals and prisons.

At first it felt kind of weird to talk through an interpreter, but it was fun. I certainly lost my fear of speaking in public! I gave my testimony several times on the street and even at a maximum-security prison where capitol punishment is still administered. Many of the inmates were in for life. I shook the hand of a murderer. Now *that* was something I'll never forget!

—Paul Donahue
Grouard, Alberta

I got to go on a mission trip to Mexico, and it changed my life! We began our first day by loading trucks with food, toys, and clothing for the poor people of Tijuana. This was weird because I saw a lot of stuff that was old and worn out—things I'd consider worthless. But when we arrived at the site and handed out these gifts, the people treated them as if they were gold!

We also spent time in an orphanage. The children were so happy to see us that they nearly plowed us over! One of their favorite toys was a wheelbarrel. They used it as a go-cart, and we all had fun pushing them in it. When we said good-bye, the children had such happy, grateful attitudes for our visit. You know what that told me? I needed to look at my priorities and what I counted as important in life.

We also visited a poor city with houses made of cardboard and sticks. One young woman lived in a wooden shack with a hole in the ground for a toilet. She had so little, yet she seemed more content than many people I know in the United States.

On the way home, most of the teens in our group weren't very talkative. Our experiences had made a life-changing effect on us, and we needed to sift through all that we'd learned. I wouldn't trade it for anything!

—Nick Marsh
Upland, California

For the past five years, my church has taken a mission trip to Sabinas, Mexico. I've been lucky enough to participate all five years. Every year we have a team that comes and fixes our meals—except on our last night. It has become a tradition for the ladies from the church in Sabinas to fix our last meal.

Their food is usually close to normal and tastes OK—except for one dish I tried a couple of years ago. I walked through the line and looked into a pot that appeared to have soup in it. When I picked up the serving spoon and stirred it, the head of a fish popped up. This definitely wasn't Long John Silver's!

We set up Bible schools at two locations. It's often well over 100 degrees outside, dusty, and swarming with mosquitoes and flies. But you know what? It's worth it all when I see children come wearing their very best clothing (which is really thin and practically shredded). Whatever inconveniences we face are worth it all to get to tell them about Jesus.

—*Bret Phillips*
*Edna, Texas*

## Mission Yucatan

**K**your
world

**AY-** *eeee!!!! Yipe! Yipe! Yipe! Eeeeeeeeeek!* The screeching echoed through the jungle making it nearly impossible to get some much-needed rest. The expedition members could only wonder which species was screaming in agony as it was being torn apart by the jaguars, now enjoying their evening meal. The ferocious growls of the vicious cats sounded much too close for comfort.

Huge, bloodthirsty mosquitoes buzzed about the netting that protected the members as they rested on hammocks hung between the vehicles. The four members sleeping on the inside were able to get restful sleep, while the two on the outside edges acted as guards and slept fitfully.

The night sounds provided an eerie backdrop as they sleepily considered what might await them at their final destination: The Yucatan

Peninsula, located at the southernmost portion of North America, deep in the heart of Mexico.

Historically, the Mayan Indians who lived there were very barbaric. Sacrificing humans to their stone gods was a common practice, and their method of sacrifice was enough to send even the bravest warrior running for home. The Mayans would cut open a living human being and pull out the beating heart to place at the feet of their stone gods. Is this how they would be thanked for delivering food, medical supplies, and Bibles? Could it be they would never actually make the return trip home?

Of course before they could discover if the tribe still practiced human sacrifices, they first had to cover several thousand miles of mud, washed out bridges, nearly impassable terrain, and the ever-present threat of road pirates waiting to ambush and rob them.

How did they get into such a predicament?

It all started when God said "I've got a little 4x4 trip in mind for you . . . "

It's been called the "ultimate 4x4 club adventure" and it truly was, with 6,200 rugged miles traversed in only 12 days. But this journey was more than just another "4x4 club adventure." And it was not just because of the terrain. It was because of the motive: To serve the Master.

Mark Krenik, 37, expedition leader and founder of Sons of Thunder 4x4 Club, wasn't living for God. As a young man his nickname was "Shark" and he was known for wild parties and fighting. After a military stint to avoid the law, he found financial success as a bouncer, a dancer for Chippendales, and model for Body Glove.

But his life never really counted for anything until he almost lost it. At age 25 he had a heart attack. Lying in the hospital emergency room, not knowing if he would live or die, the words of a street preacher he had mocked and scorned came to him. "God loves you. He sent His son Jesus to die for your sins."

By the time Mark got out of the hospital he was a saved man. Unlike many who make rash promises to God in times of desperation, Mark's conversion was real. And he began living his life for Jesus with that same dynamic passion he formerly poured into partying and trouble.

"Serving God hasn't always been easy," Mark says, "especially in the gang-infested streets of Los Angeles. I have often been beaten while sharing the gospel with those who are hurting."

But God gave him a 12-day break from the streets of Los Angeles late in 1995. As God so often does, He utilized the very things that Mark loved, motor sports and four-wheeling, and sent him on a mission.

That's how Mark, his three brothers Patrick, David, and Paul, his wife, Sandra, mother-in-law Trini Vizcarra, and their good friend Ken Stanfield, happened to be sleeping in the jungle thinking about pirates and human sacrifices.

Having prepared for this expedition for over a year, their Jeep Cherokees were well equipped to see them through the challenge. Each Cherokee was set up for a particular purpose. The navigational one was equipped with a Global Positioning System or GPS, special lighting for reading maps at night, and a custom-built tube to safely carry satellite maps.

The second vehicle held their personal items such as food, water, first-aid supplies, and camping gear. The third vehicle hauled all the mechanical concerns, including tools and spare parts. Together, the three vehicles were carrying 160 gallons of gas and the supplies that would be passed out in the Indian village.

All three Jeep Cherokees had been custom-prepared for crossing deep water. The carpet was stripped and all the crevices, screws, and doors were sealed. Bilge pumps were installed and custom-built snorkel systems were used for the engine intakes. This would allow them access across streams nearly five feet deep.

By dawn the monster mosquitoes had mostly disappeared and the group rose to continue the journey. With camp torn down and breakfast over, they hit the road, if it could be called that, by 7 A.M.

It wasn't long before they were up to their axles in mud. The going was slow as they made their way through bogs that would stretch 100 yards at a time. Although it was early, the temperature had passed the 100-degree mark.

Mud bogs are a popular 4x4 activity here in the United States both for participants and spectators. The jungle was a mud-bog lover's dream. No sooner would they successfully complete one grueling, muddy challenge than another would be waiting ahead, equal in length and difficulty. No spectators were there to cheer them on. It was man and machine motivated by a godly perseverance.

At times the vegetation and fallen logs were so thick that part of the group walked ahead to clear the path. Sweat poured from their bodies as they struggled to move heavy logs in the hot jungle. Humidity resulted from the soaring temperatures and constant rain.

Shoes and socks were saturated from the falling rain and the damp vegetation that they trudged through. "It felt like walking on wet carpet," Mark said. It left him with huge blisters on the soles of his feet, making it painful to walk.

As they struggled along, picking their way through dense vegetation and fallen logs, they came around a bend in the road and found their way blocked by close to 50 men brandishing assault rifles. But they were intellectually, physically, and spiritually prepared for setbacks such as this. Before leaving Los Angeles, the team had called Washington, D.C., to obtain information about military conflicts and guerrilla activity they might encounter along the way.

They were armed with that knowledge, an American flag, and the words of Jesus in Luke 12:11-12: *"For when they bring you before the authorities, do not become anxious about how or what to speak in your defense or what you should say, for the Holy Spirit will teach you in that very hour what you ought to say* (author's paraphrase).

They effectively communicated their mission and were allowed to pass. But the group would have several more opportunities to view assault rifles up close and personal before their journey ended.

They had more types of human encounters to be concerned about than just the militia and barbaric natives. They had also been told of the possibility of road pirates hiding in bushes along the trails that might ambush their party and rob them. In fact, documents they obtained from the United States Government included the following warning: "No route can be considered safe, although routes leading to and from Escarcega, Campeche, may be even more dangerous than others. The United States Embassy recommends against any visit or stop in Escarcega itself." Escarcega was a necessary part of their route. After much prayer, they felt God leading them to continue with their route as planned, relying on Him for safety.

What about carrying weapons? "The penalty for carrying a weapon bigger than a 9mm," Mark said, "was 30 years in jail. I asked if anyone in the group was willing to risk 30 years in jail, and we decided to trust God and leave the weapons at home."

The tactical planning that Mark learned in his military days would ensure that even if they were to encounter robbers or hostile militia men, they would not be able to "round us up like a herd of cows," according to Mark. He said they had a plan of action that would ensure at least one or two members of the group would be able to escape and go for help.

Fortunately they never encountered any road pirates; although there was a cautious awareness that it could happen at any time.

Their biggest fear was not human—it was the extremely poisonous Aullaca, or the "four-nose snake." They knew to be on the lookout for this danger, as well as others, because of extensive research and preparation that included contacting Youth With a Mission (YWAM), World Vision, and other Christian mission organizations. They also had to prepare special paperwork for themselves and their vehicles and get complete immunizations—not that an immunization would save them from the Aullaca. But God would.

At times, the group approached deep chasms that had once been covered with bridges. To get to the other side was a slow process and required extensive winching. They would work their way slowly down into the ravine. Then the winch hook would be attached to a tree or sturdy object. Inch by inch the vehicles would conquer the challenge.

After six days of some of the roughest four-wheeling that these ambitious drivers had ever experienced, they reached their destination.

Many of the villages they had planned to help had been obliterated by the recent hurricane, but two natives who visited their campsite led them to a settlement about seven miles from their original destination.

They were thrilled to find natives who had kept the faith of the early missionary explorers many, many years before. "We did run into one Indian that had never heard about Jesus Christ," Mark said. "We told him the whole story. He looked at us as if we were nuts and he went on his way. Oh well, he heard the gospel and we planted a seed. Now he's accountable. We did our job. Now we'll pray him through."

The Indians' living quarters were shelters with palm leaves for roofs. Many of them had no walls. "We were actually the only white people they had seen besides foreign archeologists," Mark said.

Beef jerky was handed out here and at many other stopping points along the way. Not understanding the meaning of the gifts, the natives were fearful of taking the food offerings and the group had, at times, to lay the jerky at the feet of the Indians. Medical supplies were also handed out. These were items the villagers had never seen before. And finally, Spanish Bibles were provided to reinforce the teaching and preaching the Sons of Thunder group members had been doing from their trucks. Even though the Indians spoke a rare Mayan dialect, Mark and his party were able to communicate well enough in Spanish. They explained what the medical supplies were used for and reassured the Indians that these items were gifts and they wanted nothing in trade for them.

"The Indians didn't know how to respond when we gave them these things," Mark said. "Nothing had been given to them before."

The group then spent several days exploring ancient Mayan ruins until it was time to hit the overgrown, washed out, mud-filled, leech and tick infested road for a nonstop journey home. Three days later they were back in Los Angeles.

Isaiah 6:8 says, "I heard the voice of the Lord saying, 'Whom shall I send?'"

Then the Sons of Thunder Christian 4x4 Club members said "Here we are, Lord; send us."

"It was a rewarding experience," Mark says reverently. "I'm going back."

This story was written by Sherri Kukla who is a freelance writer living in Chula Vista, Calif. It is used with her permission.

# 10
## So, You Wanna Go on a Mission Trip?

### Rock Your World

N ow that you've heard from teens who have been on a mission trip, maybe you're becoming interested in participating in a mission trip yourself. Remember, you don't *have* to go *anywhere* to be a missionary. You can be a missionary, rock your world, and make a difference right where you are! But if you've got a hankering for the far and wide, here are a few organizations that offer mission trips. Why not write, call, or visit their web sites to get more information?

## BRIO Missions
719-531-3400, ext. 1750
www.briomag.com
(An annual two-week international trip with
the staff of BRIO Magazine and
600 teens.)

## Youthserve
6401 The Paseo
Kansas City, MO 64131
816-333-7000, ext. 2205
Web: www.nyiyouthserve.org
E-mail: youthserve@nazarene.org
(Designed for youth groups.)

## Youth In Mission (YIM)
6401 The Paseo
Kansas City, MO 64131
816-333-7000, ext. 2210
Web: www.youthinmission.org
E-mail: yim@nazarene.org
(An eight-week summer missions experience
for college students)

## Big World Ventures
P.O. Box 703203
Tulsa, OK 74170-3203
800-599-8778
www.bigworld.org
E-mail: venture@bigworld.org

## Mercy Ships International
P.O. Box 2020
Garden Valley, TX 75771-2020
800-MERCYSHIPS or
903-939-7000
www.mercyships.org
E-mail: info@mercyships.org

## Project Serve/Youth for Christ
P.O. Box 228822
Denver, CO 80222
800-669-4932 or
303-843-6771

## Royal Servants
5401 W. Broadway
Minneapolis, MN 55428
www.royalservants.org
E-mail:
RoyalServants@Reignministries.org

## Teen World Outreach
Box 57A
Lima, NY 14485
585-582-2792
www.t-w-o.org
E-mail: two@elimfellowship.org

## Youth With a Mission
7085 Battlecreek Road S.E.
Salem, OR 97301
503-364-3837
www.ywam.org
E-mail: ywamno@compuserve.com

Are you Ready?

Before deciding to go on a mission trip, take a couple of seconds to answer a few questions, OK? Are you flexible? Are you sensitive to other cultures? Are you open-minded? Do you have a worldview?

## Interruption 3

**Turn to page 156 to take a quiz testing your Global Worldview.**

I need to warn you, though, that if you're serious about embarking on a mission trip, you've gotta be prepared. Can you imagine a physician walking into the operating room unprepared to perform surgery? That scenario could sound something like this:

Dr. Taylor: OK, people, scrub up. We've got important work to do.

Nurse Kelly: Excuse me, Dr. Taylor, but the chart doesn't specify what kind of surgery we're performing today.

Dr. Taylor: Uh . . . it's the heart. We're operating on the heart.

Nurse Kelly: What specifically will we be doing? Do I need to call for a specialist? I'm sure the anesthesiologist will also want this information.

Dr. Taylor: Kelly, that's just like you—always worrying about the specifics! Haven't you noticed my diplomas and certificates hanging on my office walls? Don't you realize that I'm more than capable of performing surgery? Don't worry about it! Let's just go. This is exciting!

Nurse Kelly: But, Dr. Taylor, there are several kinds of heart surgery! Will we be doing open heart? If so, I'll need specific equipment I wouldn't need otherwise. Or an angioplasty? Will we be doing that? Or will we be performing a valve replacement? What *kind* of heart surgery does this patient need?

Dr. Taylor: Look, Kelly! For the last time—we're going to open this guy up, operate on his heart, and stitch him closed. Now let's go!

Nurse Kelly: Dr. Taylor, I cannot in good faith—

Dr. Taylor: Oh, for goodness sakes, Kelly! I don't *know* the specific type of surgery this patient requires. I'm just going to open him up and wing it. We'll find out when we get in there.

Nurse Kelly: So this is exploratory surgery?

Dr. Taylor: No, it's definitely a serious operation. I know his heart is in bad shape. But I'm a doctor, Kelly! I can handle it!

As crazy as that sounds, it's just as ludicrous to depart for a mission trip without being spiritually prepared. *But I'm a Christian,* you may be thinking. *I can wing it! All I have to know is that Jesus forgives my sin.*

Well, actually, there's a little more to it than that. Hopefully, you're going on a mission trip because you want to help perform heart surgery for thousands of people who are dying in sin. Don't fly by feeling. Be mentally and spiritually prepared. There's a battle going on—fierce spiritual warfare. Don't dare walk into the line of fire without your armor.

# Getting Prepped

To help you prepare for the mission experience of your lifetime, here's what my friends at Big World Ventures suggest:

## Daily Bible Study and Prayer

Make sure that you're having your own quiet time with the Lord on a regular basis. You'll be your team's example, and they'll be looking to you for direction and advice. Begin searching out issues that you feel will be pertinent to the teens during their venture. Spend time worshiping the Lord and being sensitive to what He wants to do with your team.

You'll also be given the opportunity to minister at each site as you challenge the crowds to make a personal commitment to Jesus Christ. You'll need to lead them in a short prayer and take them aside to encourage them in the basics for about 15 minutes. Be prepared to do this three to five times per day. You'll then be given opportunities to have devotions with your team or with the entire group of teens.

If you're going on a mission trip with your youth group, start encouraging them *now* to spend quality time deepening their relationship with God. This, of course, includes taking time to seek Him and getting to know Him on an intimate level. You may want to go to your local Christian bookstore with them and help them pick out a devotional book to use in their quiet times with the Lord.

During the next few months, before your trip actually begins, tell your group that they can expect to grow like never before as they really begin studying the Bible in preparation for their mission venture.

Below are some foundational Bible topics to complete and discuss before the trip either alone or with your group.

1. Look inward and what do you see? (1 Samuel 16:7)
2. What do you meditate on? (Proverbs 23:7)
3. What does your heart reveal about you? (Proverbs 27:19)
4. Where are your treasures? (Matthew 6:19-21)
5. Where is God's heart? Is your heart there also? (John 3:16)

## Are You Called?

An ambassador is one who is sent on behalf of another.

1. What has Christ given you? (2 Corinthians 5:18-19)
2. What are you? (2 Corinthians 5:20)
3. Who are some examples? (Ephesians 6:20)
4. Now what is His commission? (Matthew 28:19-20)

## Righteousness/Forgiveness

Righteousness is right standing with God. It's a gift. (Romans 5:17)

1. Have you been made righteous? (Romans 3:21-26; 2 Corinthians 5:21)
2. Have you confessed your sins? (1 John 1:9)
3. Have you confessed and believed in your heart? (Romans 10:9-10)
4. Have you forgiven others? (Matthew 18:21-35)
5. Who is our righteousness? (Jeremiah 23:6; 1 Corinthians 1:30)

## Renew Your Mind

1. Is your mind new or old? (2 Corinthians 5:17)
2. Who works in you? (Philippians 2:13)
3. Where do you walk? (Psalm 1:1-3)
4. Flee *from* sin. Flee *toward* God. (2 Timothy 2:22)
5. Are you a civilian or soldier? (2 Timothy 2:4)
6. Put on the new man. (Colossians 3:10; Ephesians 4:23-24)
7. When you're new, you're dead. (Romans 6:5-7)
8. Whose mind do you have? (1 Corinthians 2:16; Philippians 2:5)

## God's Plan for Your Life

1. What kind of plans does God have for you? (Jeremiah 29:11; John 3:16)
2. When did His plan begin? (Jeremiah 1:5)
3. Does He want life or death for you? (John 10:10)
4. Be an example! (1 Timothy 4:12)

## How to Know His Will

1. We discern His will through the Bible. (2 Timothy 3:16-17)
2. Sometimes He speaks in dreams or visions. (Joel 2:28)
3. Learn to recognize His still, small voice. (1 Kings 19:12)
4. We experience peace when we follow His will. (Philippians 4:7; Colossians 3:15; John 14:27)
5. We can know His will through His Spirit. (1 Corinthians 2:10-16)

## Salvation

1. Who are the lost? (Romans 3:23; Isaiah 53:6)
2. What provision has God made? (Romans 6:23; Romans 5:8)
3. What must man do? (John 3:16; Romans 10:9-10)
4. How can one be sure? (Luke 9:23-25; 1 John 5:11-12)

## Prayer

Prayer is simply communication with God as if you were talking to a friend. We build our relationship with Jesus the same way we build our relationships with others. We spend time with Him, we share our innermost thoughts and needs with Him, and we listen to His response.

1. How do we pray? (Matthew 6:5-15)
2. Pray for His will. (John 5:14-15)
3. Pray in His powerful name. (John 14:13-14)
4. Pray with thankfulness. (Philippians 4:6)
5. Stick it out. (Hebrews 10:23, 35-39)

## Spiritual Influences

1. Are we fighting man or spirit? (Ephesians 6:10-12; 2 Corinthians 10:3-6)

2. How do we overcome?
   A. Be protected! (Ephesians 6:13-18)
   B. Whoever has the key has the power. (Matthew 16:19; 18:18-19—Bind the evil one.) Example: if you have someone else's car keys, you now have the power and authority to drive his car.
   C. Who's bigger? (1 John 4:4)
   D. Walk away from sin. (1 John 5:18; 2 Timothy 2:22-23)
3. His blood—your testimony (Revelation 12:10-11)

*Holy Spirit*
1. Who is He? (John 16:7)
   A. He's our comforter.
   B. He's our paraclete—one called alongside to help.
   C. He's a gift sent from God. (Luke 11:13)
   D. He's our intercessor. (Romans 8:26)
2. He knows the thoughts of God. (1 Corinthians 2:10-12)
3. Be consumed by God's power, His Spirit. See mighty changes and miracles in your life. (Acts 1:1-8; Romans 15:13; 1 Corinthians 2:4-5; Romans 15:17-19)
4. You're now a marked person. (Ephesians 1:13)

*God's Good Discipline*
1. Who does the Lord love? (Hebrews 12:6; Revelation 3:19; Proverbs 3:12)
2. Respect His discipline. (Hebrews 12:5; Proverbs 3:11)
3. What does His discipline produce? (Hebrews 12:11)
4. What happens when you ignore God's discipline? (Proverbs 10:17; 13:18)
5. Do you want to be blessed? (Psalm 94:12)

*Perseverance: Pushing Through the Good Times AND the Bad!*
1. How are you going to run in this life? (Hebrews 12:1; 1 Corinthians 9:24)
2. Perseverance is a testing ground for character. (Romans 5:3-4)

3. What attitude should we have while persevering? (James 1:2-4)
4. What are the results? (James 1:12)
5. What kind of life will we lead? (2 Peter 1:5-9)

## Who Is Your Strength?

1. Who was Moses' strength? (Exodus 15:2)
2. Who arms you? (2 Samuel 22:33)
3. What should be your strength? (Nehemiah 8:10) Guard this so it won't be stolen!
4. What can you do? (Philippians 4:13)
5. What energy should we use to serve? (1 Peter 4:11)

## God's Love

1. It's huge! (John 3:16)
2. Will He ever remove it? (Isaiah 54:10)
3. As Christians, can we be separated from it? (Romans 8:38-39)
4. Who does the Lord love? (Proverbs 8:17)

## Flesh Versus Spirit

1. How do you know whether you're following after the Holy Spirit or the flesh? (1 John 2:4-6)
2. Where's your mind? (Romans 8:5)
3. How does the mind after the flesh react to God? (Romans 8:7) Example: Excuses for the music we listen to, the people we hang with, or the things we do. Do we get hostile when we're told it's not of God, or do we react willingly to change?
4. What does the Holy Spirit produce? (Romans 8:6, 11)
5. What does the flesh produce? (Romans 8:6, 11)
6. What are some of the acts of the flesh? (Galatians 5:19-21)
7. What are some of the acts of the Spirit? (Galatians 5:22-25)
8. How do you walk according to the Spirit?
   A. Keep your eyes on Him at all times. (2 Corinthians 10:5)
   B. What are you thinking about? (Philippians 4:8)
   C. Don't conform to the world's standards. (Romans 12:2)
   D. Prayer keeps our minds on Him. (Ephesians 6:18; 1 Thessalonians 5:16-18)

Be a Prayer Warrior!

Other than saturating yourself in God's Word, one of the most important things you can do to prepare yourself for a mission trip is to pray. The more you pray, the stronger your prayer life will become. Here are some suggestions to get you started as you seek His guidance for your mission adventure.

## Prayer Topics:

- Favor with parents, friends, and community for support of this trip.
- The contact people in the country you'll be in.

- Finances for your trip.

- Wisdom and creativity for your youth pastor and other youth leaders on the trip.
- Pastor and leaders of your church.

- Salvation for people of the world—and particularly the country you're heading toward.
- Healing for the sick that you'll encounter in your assigned country.
- Freedom for those in your assigned country who are engaged in spiritual battle with demons.
- Health of your team members during the trip.

- Attitude of your team while in another country.

- Integrity of the leaders, team members, and contacts while in the country.
- For every team member and leader to be understanding during the trip.
- Positive Christlike change in every person in your group.

- Unity and teamwork among your group.

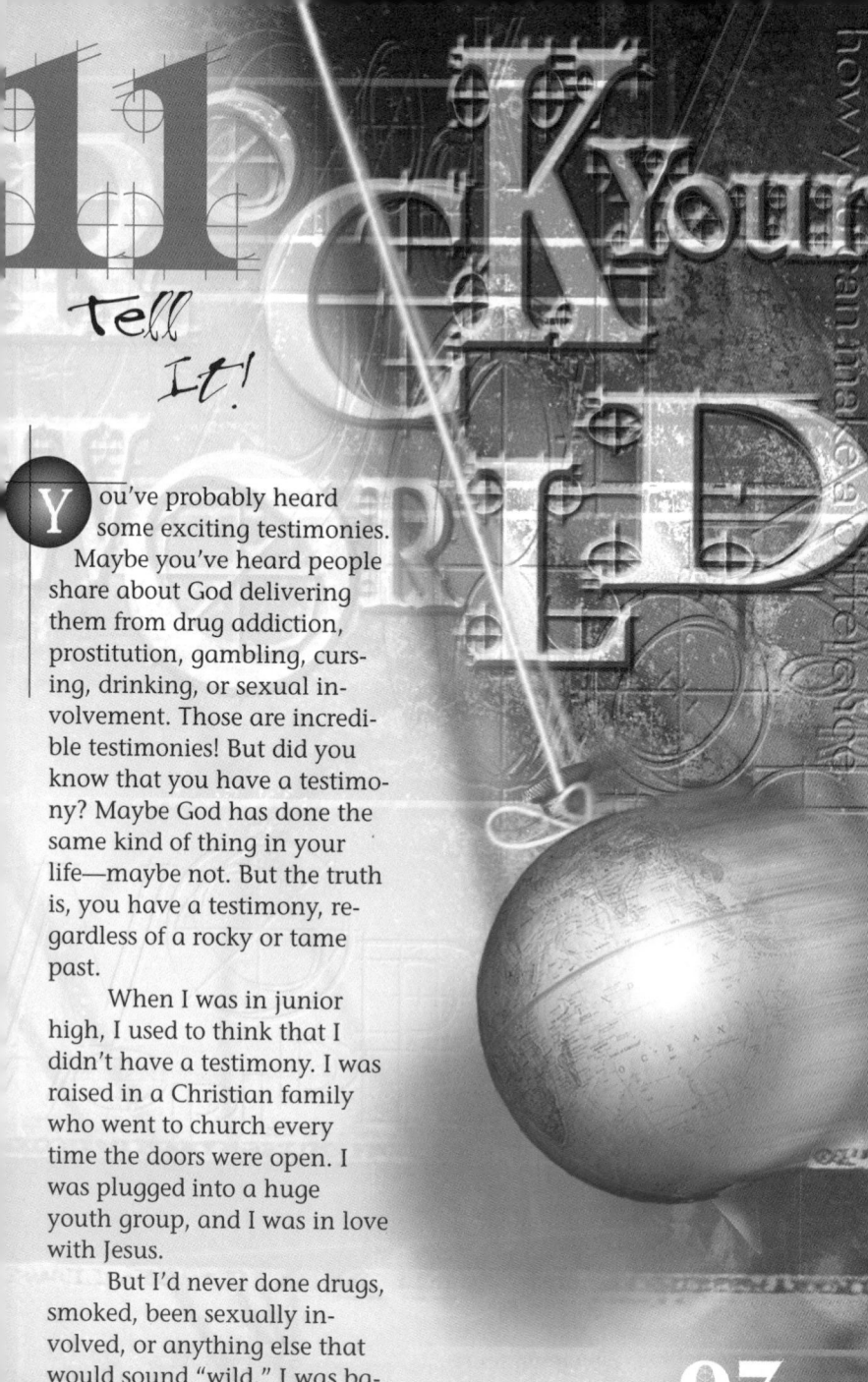

# 11

## tell It!

# ROCK your WORLD

ou've probably heard some exciting testimonies. Maybe you've heard people share about God delivering them from drug addiction, prostitution, gambling, cursing, drinking, or sexual involvement. Those are incredible testimonies! But did you know that you have a testimony? Maybe God has done the same kind of thing in your life—maybe not. But the truth is, you have a testimony, regardless of a rocky or tame past.

When I was in junior high, I used to think that I didn't have a testimony. I was raised in a Christian family who went to church every time the doors were open. I was plugged into a huge youth group, and I was in love with Jesus.

But I'd never done drugs, smoked, been sexually involved, or anything else that would sound "wild." I was basically your good kid who obeyed the rules. I loved listening to people tell about God delivering them from a wicked past. And even though I was excited for them—and amazed at God's power—it all seemed a bit foreign to me. I really couldn't relate. I'd never done any of that stuff.

It wasn't until a few years later that I began to realize I, too, had a testimony. In fact, there's something incredibly exciting about being able to say I *haven't* done any of those things—and not because *I* was so strong or capable—but simply because of God's power and grace.

So whether your past is filled with colorful stories or it's comparably calm, the fact is we were *all* born sinners. Only by God's grace and forgiveness can *any* of us be saved! Do you realize what that means? Repeat after me: "I have a testimony!"

Now that you realize you *have* a testimony, let's concentrate on putting it together, OK?

## Getting It All Together

When giving your testimony, SMILE! Be enthusiastic! Tell the audience something that you like or have enjoyed about their country. This helps them form an immediate bond with you—it brings you together through something common.

Let's begin with the basics. Write out your salvation experience in a couple of paragraphs, including the answers to the following questions. This will help form a solid foundation for what you will share with your audience.

1. When did you first hear about Jesus Christ?


2. Were you raised in a home that believed in Jesus and attended church?

3. What kind of activities have you participated in that Jesus has set you free from? (Optional)

4. When and how did you establish a personal relationship with Christ? (Example: "I was at church camp when I decided to give my heart to God." Or, "During a special youth service, I asked Christ to forgive me of my sins and come into my life." Or, "My Christian friend invited me to her church and prayed with me to accept Christ.")

5. How is your life different now that you serve Jesus compared to when you didn't?

6. What advice would you give to someone who is seeking to know what life is all about and who Jesus is?

After answering the above questions, begin to formulate your testimony. In other words, you may want to move a few paragraphs around or substitute other points of interest with the ones listed above.

Memorize it, and practice giving it to your parents and close friends. Ask them to give you some constructive criticism. For instance, are you saying "Uh, um, and a" a lot? Are you speaking too fast? Is your pronunciation and articulation clear? (This is important, because you may be speaking through an interpreter. You'll want to make it as easy as possible for him to understand you the first-time around. So enunciate!)

# Learn About Your Country

Another essential ingredient of preparation for your mission trip is to become acquainted with the country you'll be ministering in *before* you leave your hometown.

Many experiences at the ministry site will be influenced by that country's religious and cultural background. Study your country's religious and cultural background so you can prepare yourself and your team to minister more effectively.

Your local library or bookstore should be able to adequately supply you with this information. Look for a travel book about the country. A travel book will also have information regarding sites of interest, cultural foods, hot travel spots, various available restaurants, and maps of the country that may be helpful during your trip.

The more familiar you are with a country's political history, historical events, and the most recent major events, the more prepared you'll be for the trip. Learn to understand the reasons for the differences you'll experience. History books, CNN, and your local newspapers are great places to begin your education in these areas as well. The more you understand the country and the people, the more effective your ministry will be to the people who live there. Amaze everyone with your knowledge!

## Here are some research questions to get you started:

What is the primary language of this country?

How many spoken languages or dialects exist in this country?

What is the national religion?

What is the economical system like?

What form of government exists in this country?

Who is the leader of this country?

Talk It!

Another obvious way you can begin preparing for your mission trip is to learn the language of the country you'll be in. You can have a lot of fun trying to learn some basic phrases of the native language. Pick up a beginner's book and cassettes on the primary language of the country. You might also want to purchase a foreign dictionary at your local bookstore that has each word in English and the foreign word.

Here are some important words and phrases that will come in handy when an interpreter isn't around. Rewrite each English phrase in the language you'll be speaking on your mission adventure in the space provided.

1. Hi. My name is _____

2. What is your name?

3. How old are you?

4. I am _____ years old.

5. I am from _____ (fill in the name of your country).

6. Please.

7. Thank you.

8. You're welcome.

9. Where is the bathroom?

10. What time is it?

I also encourage you to learn a good portion of your testimony in the native language. When I was a college student, I spent the summer between my junior and senior year on a mission trip in the Dominican Republic, a Spanish-speaking country. Though I had never had a Spanish class, I learned some key phrases and a short version of my testimony before I left. I still remember it! And today, when I travel to Spanish-speaking countries, I'm excited to be able to still give my testimony in their own language.

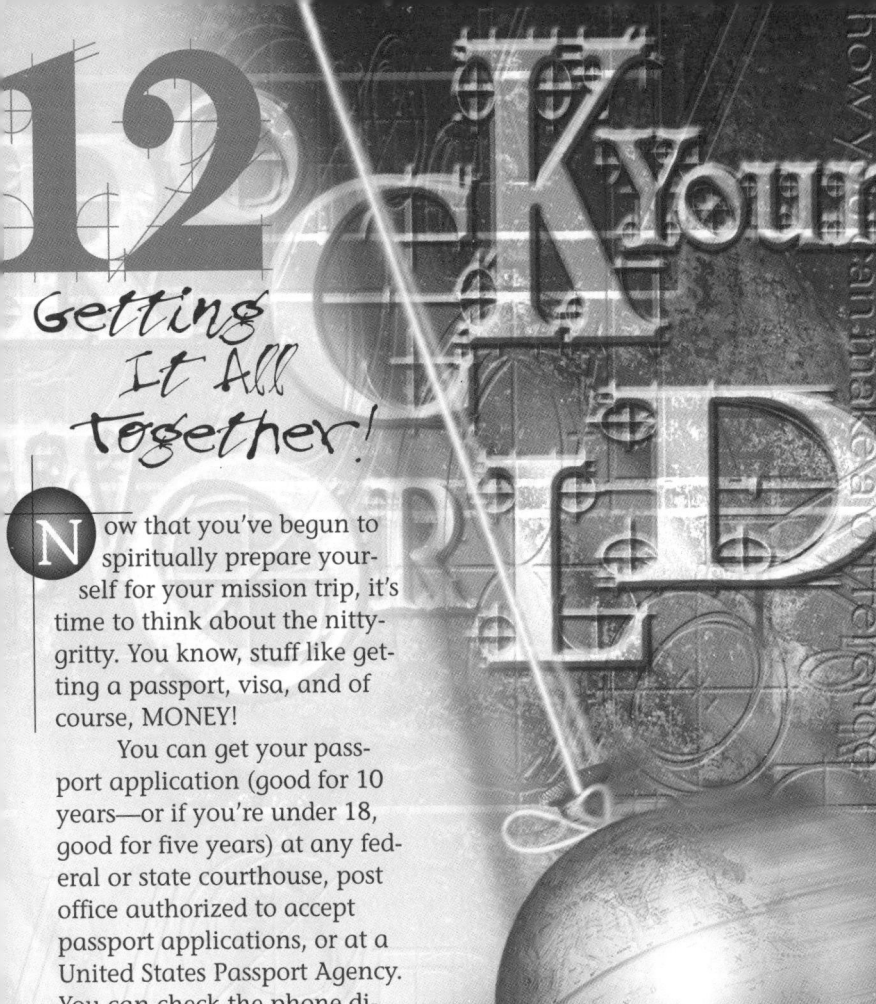

# 12

## Getting It All Together!

**N**ow that you've begun to spiritually prepare yourself for your mission trip, it's time to think about the nitty-gritty. You know, stuff like getting a passport, visa, and of course, MONEY!

You can get your passport application (good for 10 years—or if you're under 18, good for five years) at any federal or state courthouse, post office authorized to accept passport applications, or at a United States Passport Agency. You can check the phone directory under the "United States Government, State Department" section for the address.

Your passport will cost around $60 (or around $40 if you're under 16). After completing the form, you'll need to send in two passport photos (you can get two instant pictures taken for about $10 at many one-hour photo labs), your birth certificate, and the money required to process your passport. Though you'll hear that processing takes four weeks, it can sometimes take two months to get your passport back—so it's wise to apply as soon as you know you'll be involved on an overseas mission trip. If you have further questions about passports, you can call the U.S. Passport Information's 24-hour recorded message: 1-202-647-0518.

Some countries require a visa for entry and some don't. And some countries require you to obtain a visa to include in your passport. Your local travel agent can advise you on whether or not a visa is necessary.

When I took a group of teen girls to Bolivia a couple of years ago, we weren't required to have visas—only passports. But earlier this year, my dad and I went to Ethiopia, and we had to apply for a visa to be stamped in our passports before we even left the United States. When I went to Thailand, though, I simply filled out a visa application on the flight arriving in Bangkok and was granted immediate permission. Like I said, it's different with every country.

If, however, you're going to a country that requires you to have a visa in your passport before you depart from your homeland, there's a different process. In this case you'll need to fill out a visa application, send in two additional passport photos, the application fee (It's different for each country—I paid $75 for India but only $30 for Kenya), plus your passport. That's right! You'll need to mail your passport in *with* your visa application for countries requiring the visa inside your passport. They'll send your passport back with the necessary stamp inside that will allow you to enter their country.

A visa application usually takes about three weeks. Again, it's never too early to apply for a passport—especially since you may need to put it in with your visa application!

## Create a Support Base

Before you start raising support for this summer, you must be sure of one thing: God is your source! God isn't just concerned with you raising enough money to be part of summer missions; He's also deeply interested in providing, through the Church, a strong prayer support for you and an opportunity for others to take part in world evangelism.

God wants the whole world to know of His love for them. While you are raising support, you'll see God's faithfulness, and you'll be amazed at the miracles that happen!

There are so few people (or laborers) that are reaching out with His love and salvation, but the fields remain ripe and ready for the picking—if we just lift up our eyes (John 4:35, author's paraphrase).

God wants you to GO to the world, and He'll provide the finances for you to get there. You'll see that God will place it in the hearts of those in the Church to give. Guess what? He'll also nudge some of your nonbelieving friends and relatives to give! Is that hard to believe? Check *this* out, "A sinner's wealth is stored up for the righteous" (Proverbs 13:22).

Exciting, isn't it! So as you begin your fund-raising, be confident of this one thing: "With man this is impossible, but with God all things are possible" (Matthew 19:26).

## Be a Success!

Successful support bases don't just happen. Solid support bases take hard work and time, as well as a great plan. It's important to remember that people give to people. And they'll especially give to people they *know* and *trust*. Though letters are important (and we'll devote some time to this in just a second), one-on-one visits are the most effective. When you sit down with someone, look in his eyes and explain your mission—they're much more likely to respond to your need.

Besides one-on-one visits, try to line up some situations where you can speak to a *group* of people and explain your vision. For instance, seek permission to speak for 5 to 10 minutes in an adult Sunday School class at your church. Adults are bombarded with so much *bad* news about teens through the media, most of them will be overjoyed to hear you talk with your *heart* about your passion for missions.

You'll also want to send letters explaining your need. Begin with letters to your friends, family, church leadership, and then to everyone else you can think of, telling them about your mission trip.

Let them know that they're very important to the success you experience, not just financially, but by partnering with you and committing to pray for you and the ministry that you'll be involved in.

When you write this letter, remember that you're not begging for money. Your interests are in spreading the love of God to the world and taking the challenge of the Great Commission.

## Write It Down

As you compose your letter, here are some key things to include:

- Explain a little about the mission organization you're going with.
- Emphasize opportunity—not just need.

- Seek involvement and commitment.

- Realize the giver is more important than the gift. Don't pressure or manipulate!
- Explain how God has put missions in your heart for this summer.
- Tell what you'll be doing and how long you'll be there.

- Inform them on how much you need to raise each month for your payments.
- Ask if they would commit to pray for you weekly. (Have a part of your letter that they can clip out and hang on the refrigerator to remind them of their involvement.)
- Thank them for *any* involvement.

- Ask them to make their checks out to your church but send to your home address. You can then fill out a contribution form (you can get these from your church) and give it to your pastor. Many people are more willing to give when they realize their donation is tax deductible.

Here's a sample letter I created that might help you as you devise your own.

(Name)
(Address)
(Telephone number)

Dear (Name):

I'm really excited about the opportunity I have this summer to minister and serve in a unique way. I'm going on a mission trip with my youth group and (name of organization) for three weeks!

The trip begins June 11 with two days of intense training in Miami, Florida. We'll learn how to perform a 20-minute evangelistic pantomime and will give an opportunity for listeners to accept Christ at the end of the performance. We'll also learn foreign language phrases, key steps in leading someone to God, and cultural sensitivity.

From Miami, we'll fly to Rio de Janeiro, Brazil. Each day we'll minister to the Brazilians through drama in parks, prisons, orphanages, schools, churches, and streets. After each performance, we'll have the opportunity to lead the nationals into a personal relationship with Jesus Christ.

I have no doubt that God has given me this fantastic opportunity to get out of my comfort zone, see what other people believe, and share the gospel. BUT, I need to raise $1,398. This will cover the cost of my international flight, lodging, meals, and transportation within the country. I also need $285 for my domestic flight to Miami and back. I've figured I'll also need approximately $100 for snacks, emergencies, souvenirs, and offerings. That brings the total cost of my trip to $1,783.

I'm involved in several fund-raisers that will help cover part of this cost, but I'm still short. Would you consider joining me in this mission adventure by supporting me in prayer July 11 through August 1? I truly believe this is going to be a life-changing experience for both me and the people of Brazil.

If you'd like to help *more*, I'd appreciate any financial donations you feel appropriate. Please write any checks to my church (name and address) and send to my address listed at the top of this letter. I'll make sure you receive contribution credit. My final payment is due May 15.

If you're willing to commit to prayer support, financial support, or both, please let me know as soon as possible. I consider you my partner in this incredible adventure of a lifetime.

In Faith,

Susie Shellenberger

OK. Let's start talking money. Again, I checked with my friends at Big World Ventures for their suggestions. I figure since they're a full-time organization planning mission trips for individuals and youth groups, they'd probably have a stash of ideas. They did! Here's what they suggest.

*Find your friends.* You'll be surprised to find out how many are willing to help. They'll probably make you promise to write them. And you can assure them that those who support you will receive the first postcards you write from the foreign country! (But present your need in a way that lets them respond without feeling obligated. Make sure they know that every little bit helps!)

*Powerhouse of prayer.* Guess what? You can provide prayer for your ministry endeavors as well as gather financial contributions! Invite your family and friends to be part of a special evening of prayer.

Put together a really nice invitation and hand them out or mail them. Find somebody who will lead some praise and worship. Start the evening with about 20 minutes of choruses, then share your passion for summer missions and the ministry opportunities you'll have. Mention, also, the specific prayer needs you have (financial, language, health, etc.)

Have everyone gather around you and pray for you and the ministry that will take place this summer. After praying, have everyone sit down and pass out commitment cards. Write your financial and prayer needs on each card. Also include your address. Announce that they can place their cards in the box provided by the door before they leave, or they can mail them to you. End the evening with thanks and snacks.

- *Pack a pie.* Find as many people as you can to bake you a pie—all kinds of pies! Then get together with friends and take them to local businesses and sell them as gifts for a tax-deductible contribution.

- *Beg the businesses.* Well, don't actually beg. But you'll be surprised at the number of Christian-owned businesses who would love to contribute to your venture if approached in a professional manner and with materials about the trip. Remind them that all gifts are tax deductible. Ask if they'd be willing to match every dollar that you raise.

- *Church cookbooks.* Ask members of your church to share their favorite recipes. Make a cookbook with these recipes, then sell them.

- *Country Chow-Down.* Ask some moms to donate a prepared country meal (something easy like beans and cornbread). Announce it in the church bulletin and sell tons of tickets. Have a special night planned with music and skits. Shower the moms with appreciation. (Flowers can go a long way!) All proceeds will go toward funding your mission trip.

- *Cart the candy.* You'll need to get permission from your administrators for this one, but it can be very productive. Sell candy, doughnuts, hot chocolate, or cider at school. It's amazing how much 50 cents here and there can add up!

- *Clean the city.* You can really clean up with this one! Have items donated to you, advertise in the paper, and make sure you plan ahead for all the prep work. Get volunteers to price items and set out merchandise for the world's largest garage/lawn sale. If you hold the event at your church, make a big banner and consider selling soft drinks and refreshments too.

- *Special services.* Offering services for a flat fee, hourly rate, or a donation can add up quickly. The catch is—you have to be willing to work hard and do a variety of things. For instance, someone in your church might hire you to wash windows for two hours; someone else might pay you to rake leaves, haul dirt, plant a garden, clean a garage, etc.

*Clean those cars.* This one's an oldie, but it's still a goodie! Organize different teams who will wash cars on the weekends. Spread yourself out. Go to three or four great locations and have a contest seeing which group can raise the most in one day. Then have a big pizza party to celebrate. If you get tired of washing cars, call your local airport and ask if you can wash airplanes for a deal.

*Pamper the pets.* Grab some buckets, sponges, and brushes and hit the neighborhood, going house to house offering your services to wash their pet for a price or donation.

*Pledge-a-thons.* These events are what put the "fun" in fundraisers! Pledge miles, hours, or any other kind of measurement. You can get hundreds of dollars this way with a well-organized event. People are more willing to pledge when they know up front what their total commitment will be. Some will even pay in advance! But if not, you need to make sure you follow up and collect. You can do lots of good with your pledge-a-thons: work-a-thons at the church, service-a-thon with your church, witness-a-thon spending hours sharing the love of Jesus in your city, lawn-a-thon for single moms or elderly folks.

*Can it!* Area businesses can help you by donating their aluminum cans, glass and plastic bottles, and other recyclables. Meet with the store managers or owners to sell them on it.

*Pinching pennies.* If you have 10 people going house to house raising pennies for your mission trip, you'll be amazed at how much you can make! Most people will give more than a penny, and some usually give all their change and even larger donations.

# 13

## But How Do I Know?

## Rock Your World

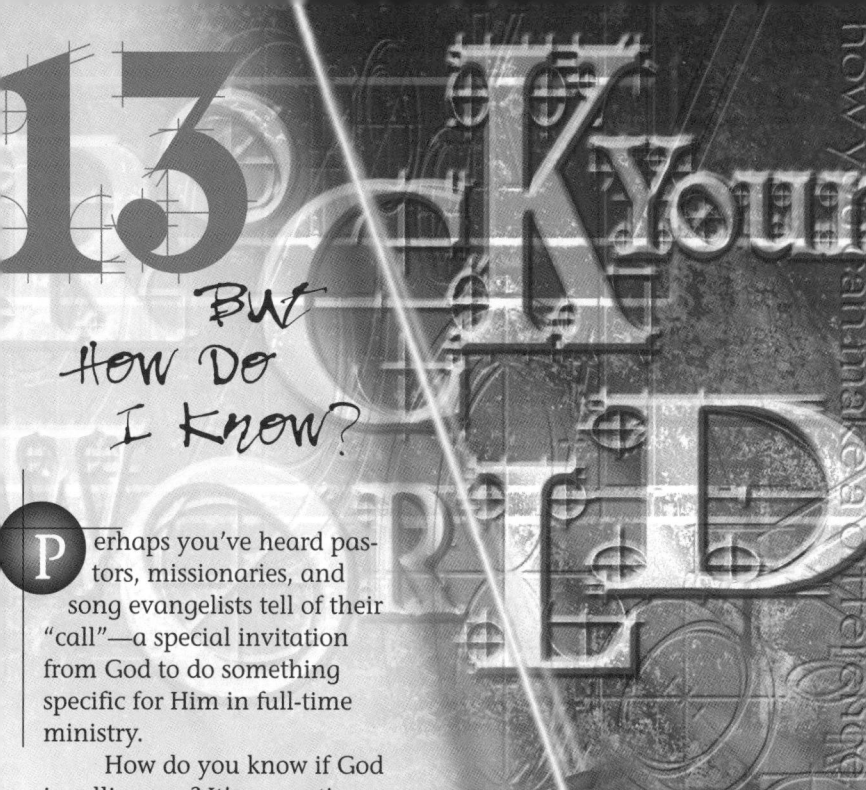

**P**erhaps you've heard pastors, missionaries, and song evangelists tell of their "call"—a special invitation from God to do something specific for Him in full-time ministry.

How do you know if God is calling *you?* It's a question worth thinking about. Chew on this: God calls ALL of us. *Some* He calls to minister through being a secretary, construction worker, clothing designer, or professional athlete. In other words, no matter what your career will be, God still calls you to minister to others, to rock your world, to make a difference in those around you.

Could God be calling *you* into full-time service? Hmmm. I called a missionary in Africa and asked her to share her story. Here's what Linda says.

# Missions: The Adventure of a Lifetime!

**by Linda Seaman**

His name was John, and he was soooo cute! Tall, broad-shouldered, dark brown eyes with lashes to kill for and a bass voice that made my heart melt. He was just as good on the inside too. Great sense of humor, sensitive, committed Christian—he was everyone's friend—and just being around him made me feel good.

He had only one flaw, but it was a major one. He had a "call" to be a missionary.

What a downer for this gorgeous, gifted, talented guy to bury himself in a jungle somewhere, never to be seen or heard from again! There was no way I was going to sacrifice *my* life and *my* dreams by being a missionary. *Forget about falling in love with him,* I thought to myself.

## Way Back When

I hadn't always felt that way about being a missionary. In fact, I grew up in a godly home where missionaries were considered to be "top of the line" Christians. When missionaries came to my church and showed their slides, I was always touched by the faces I saw and the words I heard. As the slides flashed past, I usually sat in our darkened church and cried, wondering silently if God wanted me to be a missionary.

By the time I got to junior high, though, I tried to ignore those feelings, because by then I had a much better understanding of what those missionaries did. They didn't just travel around showing neat pictures—they had to go to faraway places to take those photos —places that had huge, disgusting bugs and poisonous snakes. Places where people dressed weird and spoke foreign languages and preferred monkey stew to Big Macs.

Now, I'm no rocket scientist, but I knew this was NOT what I wanted to do with *my* life! I'd given my heart to Jesus when I was in first grade, and I wanted to do what God wanted me to do—just not on the mission field.

I figured He was probably just testing me like He did with Abraham and Isaac—you know, just to see if I was willing. But I didn't want to say yes—just in case He was serious.

# Excuse 101

I had plenty of valid arguments. I didn't play the piano, so how could I win any souls if I couldn't even plunk out "Just as I Am" for the invitation? And I'd definitely be too homesick to do any evangelism, because I really, *really*, REALLY loved my family.

In fact, I knew lots of my friends who were not getting along with their parents, so I suggested to the Lord that He call one of them. Of course, the best zinger of all was that "there are so many people right here in America who need You, God, so why go somewhere else?" (That was my favorite, because it sounded so spiritual.)

The bottom line? I didn't want to commit myself to something I knew I could never bring myself to do. I was so afraid of failing, so afraid of my inadequacies, so afraid that my life would be ruined and my hopes and dreams would go down the tubes, that I couldn't even talk to God about it. I wish I had been wise enough to *admit* my weaknesses and fears to the Lord and ask Him to change them instead of using them as excuses to avoid saying, "yes."

You see, I never really said, "no," because I certainly would never say that to God! Instead, I just stalled, avoided, and ignored. But it kept coming up. It was always there. Just when I'd be having a great time spiritually, up it would come—this missionary thing— and I'd shut myself off from God rather than deal with it.

# Perfect Plans

Finally one night, when I was a junior in high school, I lay in bed thinking about my future. I had it all planned. I'd go to a Christian college and meet a great Christian guy (someone just like John, only without THE CALL). We'd get married, move back to my hometown, I'd teach for a while, and then we'd have children who could grow up surrounded by their loving, extended family.

We would go to church faithfully and be strong, supportive laypeople (just as my family had been for three generations), and everything would be PERFECT.

Then the Lord spoke to my heart and said, "Yes, Linda, but you know that I want you to be a missionary." I somehow knew in that moment that the time had come to make a decision.

There wasn't anything wrong with my picture—not one thing sinful about what I wanted to do with my life—EXCEPT that it wasn't what God wanted.

In my darkened bedroom, I felt God's presence. He was *extremely* close. I heard Him say, "I will never force you to do this, Linda, but you must understand that if you choose your way over mine, at all the moments in your 'perfect' future that bring you great happiness, you will say to yourself, 'Yes, but I wonder what *might have been* if I had done what God wanted me to do.'"

I knew then that I could never be content with second best. I grabbed my Bible off the night stand, opened it, glanced down, and read these words from Matthew 10:37-39 that I had already underlined:

> If you love your father and mother more than me, you are not worthy of being mine; or if you love your son or daughter more than me, you are not worthy of being mine. If you refuse to take up your cross and follow me, you are not worthy of being mine. If you cling to your life, you will lose it; but if you give it up for me, you will save it (TLB).

I knew that those were God's words to me. So I finally, *finally* said, "YES" to Him.

## Change of Heart

Have you ever read the Dr. Seuss book *Green Eggs and Ham?* Remember good old Sam-I-Am, who does his best to convince his friend to try green eggs and ham? His pal isn't as stupid as he looks, though, and refuses, knowing without having actually tasted them that he'd hate them.

But Sam-I-Am is very persistent. So finally, just to get Sam off his back, his buddy agrees to try them. We all know that he discovers, much to his surprise, that he actually *loves* green eggs and ham.

Well, that pretty much describes how I feel today. After all those years of resisting because I thought I knew what was best for me, I have discovered that saying, "Yes," to God was the smartest thing I ever did! I absolutely *love* being a missionary and wouldn't trade places with anyone. How thankful I am that God didn't give up on me and say, "Fine, You don't want to go—I'll find someone who does!"

Through the years, I've learned that God wants my happiness even more than I do. And guess what? I even got to marry John! We have three great kids, have traveled all over the world, lived in the Caribbean and Africa, and we have wonderful friends of many different nationalities.

Best of all, though, I've had the privilege of taking the gospel to those who have never heard it before and have seen people's lives *transformed* by the power of God!

## Wanting God's Will

Most missionaries I've met always wanted to be missionaries, and they never struggled over their call. I *have* met a surprising number of people over the years, though, who have told me that God called them when they were young, but they chose another path instead and have always regretted it.

Esther 4:14 tells us that God will get His work done with or without you, but if you don't do what He asks, YOU will be the loser. So, in the words of a missionary friend of mine, "If God is calling *you* to be a missionary, cancel the pity party and start the celebration!"

*"Missions: The Adventure of a Lifetime," by Linda Seaman, first appeared in the January 1996 issue of Brio magazine. Linda and her husband, John, have three children and are missionaries for the Church of the Nazarene in Ivory Coast, West Africa. This story is used with the author's permission.*

*Recipe for Growth*

Is God calling *you* to be a missionary? Well, in a sense, He calls *all* of us. Some He sends overseas, and others He keeps at home. But wherever you live, and whatever your career will be, God still wants to use *you* as a light.

In order for you to shine effectively, you need to be growing spiritually. Reading your Bible and praying on a daily basis are the two most important steps you can take to strengthen your spiritual life. Some people call this devotions. You might call it your special time with the Lord. God isn't concerned about what it's called—He's just concerned that you do it.

Since spiritual growth is *daily* activity, let's use the word *daily* as a recipe for growing closer to Jesus.

**D:** *Don't compromise.* With the Holy Spirit's help, you *can* say no to temptation. When you're pressured to cheat, claim His strength and say no. When you're tempted to watch a television show or movie that's sexually suggestive, violent, or goes against God's standards in any way, refuse.

Living a life of no compromise doesn't mean you're perfect. But it *does* mean that you're 100 percent committed to the Lordship of Jesus Christ.

**A:** *Ask for daily opportunities to share His love.* You serve a God of a million possibilities. He's more excited than you can imagine to influence others through you! When you ask Him to bring someone across your path who needs Him, He'll respond.

As soon as you've asked Him to do this, start thanking Him ahead of time! Then be on the lookout all day for that one person. And don't be afraid. God's not going to turn you into a religious fanatic or make you be someone you're not. He'll use your own personality—the special way He created you—to make a difference in someone's life.

*I:* *Realize your* **importance.** YOU are very important to God, and He wants to do important things through you. The faster you realize this, the sooner you'll become more confident in His desire to use you to make a difference. Never worry about what you can't do. God is the one who equips. He'll never call you to do something without providing everything you need to do it. You see, God isn't concerned about your *ability*—He's concerned about your *availability.*

*L:* **Live** *the life.* Did you know that the strongest testimony a missionary has is his or her own lifestyle? With that in mind, you can actually be a missionary right now! By living a Christlike lifestyle, you can be a life-sized Bible to the world around you.

Does this mean you always have to have a Scripture on your tongue? No. It *does* mean that your lifestyle should be so attractive that others will want what they see. If you're always complaining and looking for the negative side of life, people won't want your attitude. Strive, instead, to wear a smile and encourage others. This kind of positive attitude is what magnetizes people to you.

*Y:* **Yes,** *Lord!* Let this be your life's motto. Be willing to say, "Yes, Lord," to anything He asks of you—anytime and anywhere.

# 14

## Sometimes It Hurts

**I**t's easy to take the privileges of going to church and expressing our faith for granted. Even though it's easy for most North Americans, there are *some* places in the world where it's extremely dangerous to be a Christian. Check out *these* facts:

- More Christians died for their faith in the 20th century than in the previous 19 centuries combined.
- In Sudan, thousands of Christian children have been snatched from their homes and sold into slavery.
- In Saudi Arabia, conversion to Christianity is against the law and punishable by death.

- In February 1996, a mob of more than 10,000 Muslims pillaged and burned three Christian villages located in the Nile Delta.
- In Nigeria, approximately 6,000 people (mostly Christian) have been killed since the 1980s. This was due to interreligious clashes.
- In China there are more Christians in prison for their faith than in any other country in the world.
- Several Americans have been arrested in China and Vietnam for practicing Christianity outside of government control.
- More than one million (mainly Christians) have died in religious wars in Sudan within the last few years.
- Christians around the world are suffering cruelties such as amputation, bombings, crucifixion, displacement, flogging, kidnapping, murder, prison, rape, and slavery.
- The main countries involved in Christian persecution are Sudan, Pakistan, Saudi Arabia, Egypt, Nigeria, Uzbekistan, China, North Korea, Vietnam, Cuba, and Laos. Most of these countries have strong trade agreements with the United States.

Most of us don't realize how good we have it! Think about it: We can choose the church we wish to attend. We can get involved in as many ministries and activities in our churches and with our youth groups as we want. We can go to church as often as the doors are open. We don't have to worship in secret. We can sing loudly and praise God openly.

Because we North Americans have it so easy, it's hard to even *imagine* what real persecution is like. Are you ready for a clear picture? Read on!

# A Father and Son

*Millions of Christians around the world are being persecuted because of their beliefs. Who will hear their cries?*

In the middle of this century, during the communist revolution in China, a missionary and his son were captured by communist soldiers, who threatened to kill the son unless the father denied his faith.

He would not.

The soldiers beat the son as the father looked on in disbelief. The military officer smiled and said, "Now will you deny this Jesus?"

"Oh, God!" the missionary cried to the ceiling. His heart wrenched, his eyes glazed over in tears, and his face tightened. Staring at the floor, he whispered, "No, I will not deny Him."

The soldiers began to torture the boy. "Save me, Daddy! Save me!" the boy pleaded.

The father's knees failed and he slumped to the floor. "No . . . Jesus . . . Please, Jesus, no. I will not deny my faith!"

Later, the father and the son both were killed by the soldiers. However, they died knowing that they had not denied Jesus as their Lord and Savior.

This story is adapted from Peter Marshall's book *Their Blood Cries Out* (Nashville: Thomas Nelson, 1997), 173-74.

## Real-Life Horror

This did not happen in the movies. It's not a fictional account. It's true. It happened.

More frightening than that, it is not an isolated case. In fact, a greater number of Christians have died for their faith this century than in the previous 19 centuries combined. Four hundred Christians will die today. And most churches in the West don't know or aren't doing anything about it.

Organizations such as Freedom House and the World Evangelical Fellowship are attempting to educate people about religious persecution worldwide. Here's a sampling of six countries where believers are under extreme attack.

*China:* Traveling at night, preaching and speaking during the day, pastors of house churches in China work in dangerous surroundings. Protestant and Catholic Christians alike have been arrested, imprisoned, and even killed. More Christians are imprisoned for their faith in China than in any other country in the world.

*Pakistan:* The rise of Islamic fundamentalism is turning the once tolerant Muslim faith into a brutally repressive force. Those who worship Christ are increasingly accused of blasphemy against Muhammad. If convicted, Islamic law calls for the death sentence. In some cases, crowds have beaten and killed people who haven't been formally accused and tried or have been declared innocent in court.

*Sudan:* This nation is wracked by civil war, and Sudan's totalitarian government has allied itself with Islamic extremists to declare a holy war against Christians and other non-Muslims. The resulting reign of government-endorsed terror has resulted in the deaths of more than a million people and the forced displacement of more than three million, whose homes and villages have been burned and whose property has been confiscated. The abduction, imprisonment, torture, and execution of men break up Christian families. Women and children are kidnapped, sold into slavery for as little as $15, and forced to work as slaves or concubines for their Muslim masters.

*North Korea:* The government of this, the only remaining Stalinist country in the world, has not only attempted to stamp out Christianity but also established an official state religion that requires the worship of the nation's leaders. By the early 1960s, all church buildings were closed and all Bibles were destroyed. Clergy and religious leaders were executed or sent to concentration camps. As a result, the Christians who remain practice their faith in secrecy—always in danger of losing their lives.

*Saudi Arabia and Egypt:* Even in nations that have aligned themselves politically with the West, the spread of a militant strain of Islam

rock your world

has led to the persecution of those who practice the Christian faith. In Saudi Arabia, conversion to Christianity is a crime punishable by death, and those who worship Christ may lose all their property, be fined, imprisoned, and exiled. In Egypt, the government has turned a blind eye to the persecution of Coptic and evangelical Christians.

## One Body

See any differences in how you practice your devotion to Jesus Christ compared to Christians in those countries? Stupid question, right?

If you live in the United States or Canada, your church services are probably performed in air-conditioned, well-kept sanctuaries. The music rings, voices sing, and the pastor boldly proclaims the Good News of Jesus Christ.

But in countries such as Nepal, Iran, and Cuba, Christians sneak to village church services, always afraid that they'll be found out. Others huddle together as families and read a tattered Bible that has to be hidden during the week. Still others wake up in prison.

Religious persecution affects 200 million people in more than 60 countries, with an additional 400 million suffering from discrimination and legal impediments.

If what you're reading doesn't shock you, check your pulse. If you're breathing, you should be bothered.

If what you've just learned doesn't turn your stomach, check your antacid. It must be a good one, because if you're alive you should be tied in knots.

And if discovering that Christians are being harassed, tortured, killed, displaced, and discriminated against doesn't bring about some righteous anger, check your heart. If you're a believer, you better be compassionate to those who suffer for the faith.

The Bible is clear:

*There should be no division in the body, but its parts should have equal concern for each other. If one part suffers, every part suffers with it; if one part is honored, every part rejoices with it* (1 Corinthians 12:25-26).

*Remember those in prison as if you were their fellow prisoners, and those who are mistreated as if you yourselves were suffering* (Hebrews 13:3).

## What Can I Do?

While you may be ready to hop on a plane and do your best Rambo imitation to save persecuted Christians in foreign lands, the best thing you can do is pray.

Yes, pray. Prayer is more powerful than any of us will ever realize. Only God can change hearts, dethrone rulers, and alter the cultural climate that oppresses believers around the globe. And God *does* listen to His people.

### Here are some ideas for prayer:

1. Thank God for the faithfulness of persecuted believers.

2. Pray for the spouses, children, and families of persecuted Christians.

3. Pray for the provision of Bibles and other Christian literature.

4. Pray for God to raise up more leaders among the persecuted church.

5. Pray for the oppressors of Christians, that they may experience repentance and salvation.

6. Take a day to pray specifically for the persecuted Christians in China, Pakistan, Mongolia, Mexico, Peru, Turkey, Iran, Egypt, Nigeria, Sudan, Greece, Bulgaria, Vietnam, and North Korea.

7. Pray that leaders in democratic countries will have the courage to speak out regarding this violation of human rights.

8.  Pray that Westerners, especially Christians, will be aroused and no longer tolerate the persecution of members of Christ's Body.

You can make a difference.

**For further information on religious persecution contact:**

**Voice of the Martyrs**
P.O. Box 443
Bartlesville, OK 74005
www.persecution.com
E-mail: thevoice@vom.usa.org

**Christian Solidarity International**
U.S. Office: 870 Hampshire Road
Suite T
Westlake Village, CA 91361
www.csi-int.ch
E-mail: csi@csi-usa.org

For further information on Christian persecution, you can obtain the following book from your local Christian bookstore: *In the Lion's Den.*

Warning: Many accounts of persecution in this book have violent content and may not be suitable for younger readers.

*Most of the information in this chapter came from the **Voice of the Martyrs** and is used with permission.*

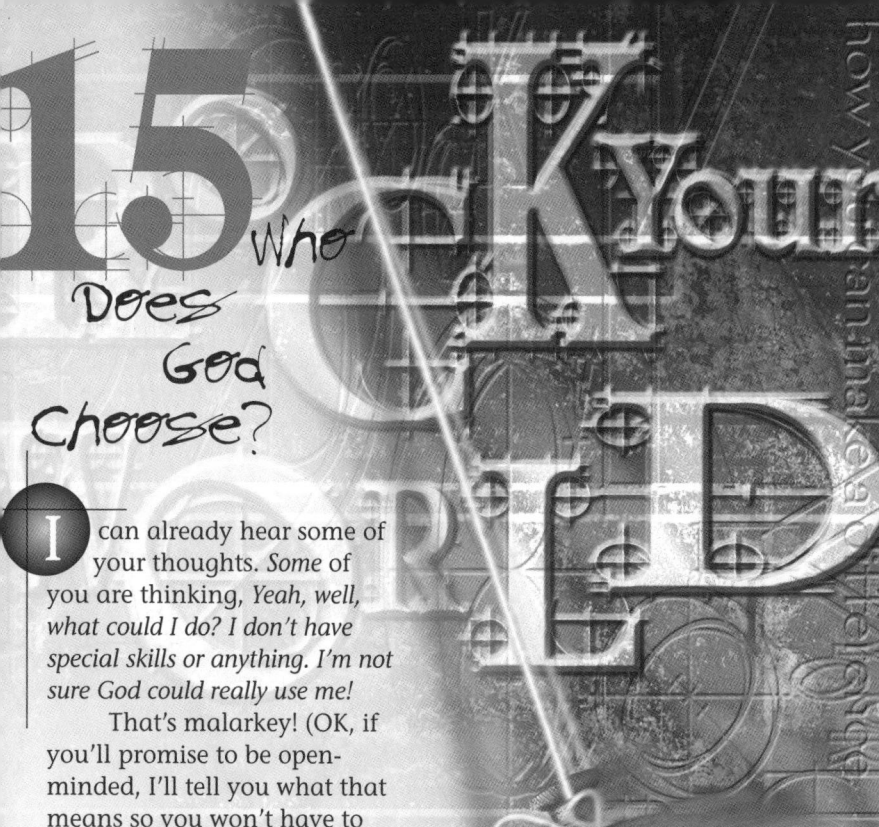

# 15

## Who Does God Choose?

I can already hear some of your thoughts. *Some* of you are thinking, *Yeah, well, what could I do? I don't have special skills or anything. I'm not sure God could really use me!*

That's malarkey! (OK, if you'll promise to be open-minded, I'll tell you what that means so you won't have to go look it up. It's nonsense. But keep the Webster's handy, just in case I decide to throw in another word I learned from playing the dictionary game.)

Just what kind of person does God choose?

The lovely? The talented? The one who's popular and outgoing? The girl who makes everyone feel welcome and wanted when they're around her? The guy who's smart and crafty and can build his own computer or toss a football across the country?

Maybe.

Maybe not.

But God doesn't choose you on your *abilities.* He chooses you on your *availability.* See, the issue is *not* how good, smart, pretty, handsome, cool, or popular you are. The issue is: Are you available?

If you are, God chooses *you!* The Bible is jam-packed with incredible examples of people who had zero ability, but God used them in mighty ways to change history and people—simply because they were *available.*

Are you catching the picture, seeing the vision? God chooses YOU! He wants to use you. And He doesn't just want to use you a little bit. He wants to do things in and through you that are far beyond your imagination! Way beyond what you could ever dream up—God wants to do more!

Exciting, isn't it?

You are a pur sang choice of God's. (Ha! Told you to hang on to that dictionary. It's an adjective that means beyond a doubt—to the utmost degree.) In other words, God wants to use *you* to the ultimate degree. The question is, will you let Him?

Instead of worrying about what you *can't* do, let me challenge you to concentrate, instead, on allowing God to make the difference. You see, whatever you lack, He can supply!

---

## Meet Greta!

Let me introduce you to someone who can back me up. Twenty-year-old Greta Anspach is from Van Wert, Ohio. She doesn't hold a college degree. She's had no language training. And she's never been trained in educational strategies and objectives. *But* she's a full-time teacher!

I guess I'd better back up, huh?

Two years ago, Greta was an outdoor guide at Phantom Ranch Bible Camp in Mukwonago, Wisconsin. She was hired to lead canoeing, rock climbing, bike trips, and white-water rafting. Well, she ended up doing all of that *plus* cooking, giving devotions, counseling, driving buses, teaching, and leading music.

"It was so outrageous!" she says. "Only God could equip me to do so many things I wasn't trained for. I figured He must have a reason He wanted me to learn these things. So I decided to be flexible and allow Him to stretch me."

Greta learned first-hand that she could do all things through Him who gave her the strength. And even though she had a fantastic summer working at camp, there was still that nagging question of what she'd do in the fall.

*God, what do You have for me?* she often wondered. *How can You use my love of the outdoors and adventure to bring glory to You?*

## Greta Meets Marta

Not long after praying this prayer, a missionary came to Greta's home church. Marta is Ethiopian but lives part of each year in Indiana. She and her husband, Demi, founded Project Mercy—a mission organization striving to make a difference in remote areas of Ethiopia.

Greta was captivated with Marta. She told colorful stories. She spoke humbly, yet boldly, about the great need of the Ethiopians. She especially focused on one particular area of Ethiopia—an area so remote that no school had ever been started. None of the children could read or write. People were starving. They needed to learn how to productively grow and nurture crops. They needed basic sanitation and nutritional help.

Greta's heart was moved. And God began to work. *Ethiopia? But I don't even have a college degree,* she thought. *What could I do? How could God use me?*

And then she remembered all He had helped her learn at camp. *I didn't know how to fix bicycles or drive a bus,* she mused. *But God came through. I was successful—not because I had the ability—but because I allowed Him to equip me with what I needed.*

Greta told God she was ready to be used. She approached Marta and Demi and was soon accepted to become the first female American teacher for Project Mercy. *And* at the very first school Project Mercy had launched. *And* in an area so remote they couldn't even call it a village. It was more like a valley with people scattered in the mountains, between trees, and along dirt roads.

# Into Africa

A few months later, Greta was in Ethiopia. "I raised my support for an entire year," she says. "Project Mercy provides my housing here at the school, and my support money goes for food and personal items. I really don't need much money. Last month I spent $30, and that was because I went into Addis Ababa (the capital) and bought a dictionary and two maps."

Because Ethiopia is predominately made up of Muslims, missionaries had never been welcome in the remote valley that Greta was now living in. "We call it the Yetebon Valley," she says. "And it's been so impoverished, largely due to the fact that the Muslims didn't want the missionaries invading this area. In fact, they ran off many of the missionaries. The Muslims would throw rocks at them and try to stone them.

"I think the reason they've accepted Marta and Demi," she says, "is because they're Ethiopian. Even though they're Christians, the Muslims see them as family."

# Back to the Basics

The school is now in its second year of operation and has 430 students, with more than 1,000 still on the waiting list. There are mothers who bring their children to the doors of the school *begging* to have them educated. They leave crying because there simply aren't enough teachers or space.

"These kids know what a privilege it is to go to school," Greta says. "They never had school. They knew absolutely nothing. We had to teach them how to hold a pencil. When we handed out paper, they didn't know what the lines were for. They held their books upside down. But they're so excited to be learning! They're so grateful to be in school."

Children who live in the mountains walk as far as three hours each morning and three hours each afternoon to and from school. Do they complain? No way! They come down the mountain *singing!* And even though the students are from Muslim homes, they love school so much that they often hang around after hours to join in on the optional Bible studies. The result? *Hundreds* of children and their parents have accepted Christ as their personal savior!

## Multiplying the Workers

Greta taught for a year in the Yetebon Valley then returned to Ohio for the summer. She was so excited about what God was doing in her life and with the children, she was able to convince one of her best friends who had just graduated from college to join her as a new teacher for Project Mercy.

"I was really interested in doing some kind of short-term mission work," 21-year-old Bethany Fegley says. "My mom has always told me that the safest place to be is in God's will. I love it here! The children are so excited to learn. Even though we see them every Monday through Friday, each time I walk through the door of the classroom, they gasp! They're just on the edge of their seats!"

And they really *are* on the edge of their seats. I recently visited Greta and Bethany in the Yetebon Valley, because I wanted to get an up-close look at what they are doing. Seventy kids are crammed into one classroom and sit three to a desk. It's hot and sometimes stinky, but no one complains.

I watched Bethany teach art. I brought several cartons of colored markers with me to give her for classroom supplies. "These will be great for today's project!" she said. "We've just made paper airplanes. The kids have never seen them before. They're so excited!"

I grabbed my camera and watched as she took them outside and taught them how to fly their new creations. They squealed with delight as paper took to the air. When they went back inside to decorate their planes with the brand-new markers, the kids were ecstatic!

"I tried not to laugh out loud," Bethany says. "But I didn't realize they wouldn't know how to use them. They didn't know they were supposed to take the cap off, and they couldn't figure out why nothing was coming out. They smelled them and gasped in wonder as the bright colors shone on the paper."

# A Little Goes a Long Way

I wandered into Greta's classroom and interrupted her English lesson. All 70 students stood and greeted me in their best English. "Gude mowneen!" they shouted.

"Don't mind me," I said. "I'll just try not to disrupt you guys, OK?" (As if a white girl with a camera around her neck could be inconspicuous!)

Greta held up a large bag with several items in it. She was teaching the students a variety of English phrases. "Is there a book?" she asked.

"Is there a book?" they repeated.

She then reached inside and pulled out a book. "There IS a book!"

"There IS a book!" they responded.

She went through several other items, then mischievously caught my eye. Wondering what would happen next, I continued to observe. She reached into the bag and pulled out a raccoon puppet. The children exploded in excitement.

"Is there a raccoon?" she asked.

"Is there a raccoon?" they repeated.

"There IS a raccoon!" she answered.

"There IS a raccoon!" they responded.

She teased a few children by gently nosing the puppet into their dirty little faces, then placed him back inside the bag.

"That was great!" I commented after class. "They sure love that puppet, don't they?"

"They do now," she said. "But it took them a while."

"What do you mean?" I asked.

She explained, "At first, they thought it was real. You've got to remember these kids have never been exposed to simple luxuries that we often take for granted. Just last week one of my students waited for me after class and said, 'Teacher, what do raccoons eat?' I tried to name a few things that I assumed were right. But he looked me right in the eyes and said, 'No, teacher. Raccoons eat arms!' I've had to teach them it's just pretend. They know now that this puppet is something we have fun with."

# Learning = Doing

The school just recently completed a small building with toilets and showers. "We've had to teach them basic sanitation," Marta explains. "Just last week we had mock shower and toilet drills. They didn't know how to use the toilet or take a shower, so we walked them through our building before we opened it for use. We explained how to take a shower and get yourself clean, and we also taught them why it's important to use a toilet. Now, once a week, every child is on a rotation and gets to take a shower when he or she arrives at school."

The teachers at Project Mercy are teaching the students that even though they're accustomed to using the bathroom out in the bushes, it's much better *not* to because that's what attracts flies. The insects hover around the human waste, pick up germs, and then spread them to the people. Several families have children with tuberculosis due to unsanitary conditions.

Though it's impossible for these folks to ever be able to build or afford a toilet, the teachers encourage the children to go home and convince their parents to dig a deep hole beyond their hut—and that becomes their toilet. The result? The spread of disease is slowed down because the human waste is not so accessible to the insects.

Every day at noon, the children receive a carrot and a piece of bread as a midday snack. When I was there, the headmaster walked into the classroom I was visiting, held up a carrot, began talking in Amheric (the Ethiopian language), and started eating.

I asked Greta what he was doing. "We've just started giving the children carrots," she explained. "They've never eaten them before. This is a new vegetable to them. They think you're supposed to eat it like corn on the cob. They've been chewing around the outside of the carrot and leaving the entire middle of it uneaten.

"Our headmaster is showing them that it's OK to eat the entire carrot—that it's nutritional for them and it tastes good too."

The exciting part? Project Mercy is teaching the students how to grow carrots and is sending them home with seeds. The children are now sharing that knowledge with their parents, and they're growing rows of carrots behind their huts.

# God Makes the Difference

Bethany never dreamed she'd walk away from a prestigious job opportunity after college graduation and live in a valley so remote that there is no phone, TV, or other modern convenience.

And Greta—without a college degree—never imagined she'd be teaching English and music to children who had never even seen pencils before!

But you see, that's where God comes in! Whatever we lack—whether it's a degree, skill, or courage—He supplies in abundance! Remember that it's not our *ability* He's concerned with. It's our *availability!*

How can God use you? The truth is, the sky's the limit! He wants to do far beyond what you could ever dream!

You're probably not in a position to head to the mission field right now. But you can still be involved. How? By praying! I believe every single prayer we pray makes a difference. Will you pray for the students and teachers of Project Mercy? More than 1,000 students are on the waiting list to enter school. Pray for God to send more teachers. Ask Him to provide more funding so additional classrooms can be built.

And consider getting involved financially. Marta says it costs $30 a month for each student to receive clothing, food, education, and supplies in the Yetebon Valley school that Project Mercy is operating. For $30, you could provide all that for one child's entire month. OR you could provide an entire year of schooling.

Can't afford that? OK, let's break it down to even simpler terms. Ten dollars will buy 40 lbs. of carrots. That 40 lbs. will feed 430 kids—the entire student body—snacks for one day. Unbelievable, isn't it? Will you prayerfully consider ways that *you* can help?

**Project Mercy**
7011 Ardmore Avenue
Fort Wayne, IN 46809
260-747-2559

# 16

## Check Your Commitment

**K Your WORLD**

W e've talked about several ways you can change your world, but remember way back at the beginning of the book when we chatted about commitment? *That's* really the key! You cannot make an eternal difference in anyone's life, unless you're totally sold out to Jesus Christ.

Let's talk about it one more time. I'll make it really easy to understand by putting the whole thing in the form of a parable, OK?

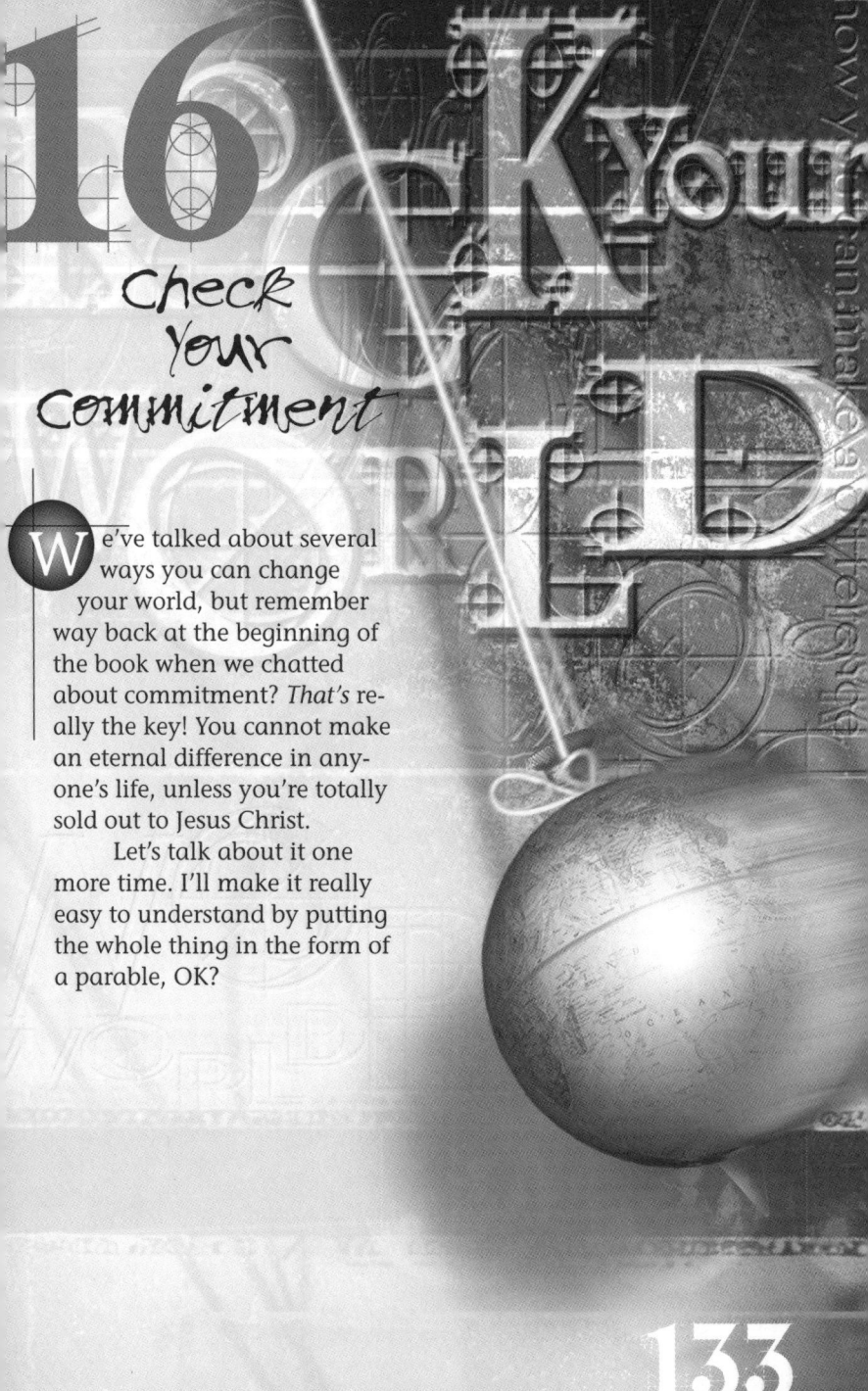

## The House

## A parable on total commitment

Amber lived alone in a big, beautiful house. At first she enjoyed it; she swam in the heated Olympic-sized pool in the gym, she studied in the vast library, and she piled her closets high with both her clutter and her most prized possessions.

But lately Amber had noticed she was feeling lonely and empty inside the house. Much of it was still unexplored because it was so big. At night, some parts of the house even frightened her. She knew some things around the house needed fixing, but she wasn't sure how to start.

So one day Amber went to the designer and builder of the house. He had overseen the construction of every inch of Amber's home. "I love the house you've built," she said. "And I'm having a lot of fun in it. But, well, something's just not right. I don't know." Then she paused and twisted the ends of her hair. "It's like something is missing."

The designer didn't say anything. He just studied Amber's face and listened as she continued. "I've decorated and rearranged the rooms a hundred different ways, but nothing I do seems right," she said. "Since you're the designer, I figure you'd know better than anyone how best to arrange my home. After all, you built it."

After some discussion, Amber decided to invite the designer to move into her house and show her how to get the most out of it. "I'm tired of feeling lost in my home," she explained. "Sometimes I can't even find my way around."

## Roomies

After the designer moved in, Amber placed a few restrictions on him—just in case he might tamper with specific things she wanted left alone.

"You can sleep in that room over there," she directed. "No," he argued. "*You* sleep in there. *I* want the master bedroom."

"Oh, no!" Amber shouted. "You can't! That's *my* room. And another thing: Don't do any remodeling in my gym, don't use the pool, don't handle my CD collection or stereo equipment, and stay away from my computer."

Before the designer could respond, Amber continued. "You can help with the yard work, but leave the cooking to me. I'm very picky about what I eat and know exactly what I want. Oh, yeah, and don't *ever* go into my bedroom closet. It holds my most prized possessions—plus a list of all my dreams and plans for the future. Other than that, feel free to make yourself at home."

# What's Happening?

So the designer and Amber began to live together in the big house. It was obvious someone had moved in. The house seemed a little different now. Even the neighbors had noticed the change.

But after a few months, Amber approached the designer. "I invited you into my house because I was lonely. I needed someone to help me keep my home organized and arranged properly. I also thought you'd show me the best way to use it, but I still feel like I'm going in circles."

The designer shifted the tool belt around his waist and motioned for Amber to sit on the stairs with him. "I know this house better than *anyone* because I made it. I know every doorway and window and even the number of bricks in the walls," he said. "I could do so much for you, but you've boxed me in. You've laid so many restrictions on me, it's almost impossible for me to do anything for you."

Amber felt uncomfortable. *Maybe that's true,* she thought. *But it IS my house!* The designer interrupted her thoughts. "Give me complete freedom—absolute control," he said, "and I'll show you how to get the very best out of this home."

# Building Trust

They talked a while longer, and over a cup of hot chocolate, Amber decided to take the designer up on his offer.

The first thing the designer did was move into the master be[d]room and put Amber into one of the guestrooms. Then he asked to let him see in her secret closet. Amber struggled, reminding the designer that the closet held all her dreams, goals, and everythin[g] importance to her. But the designer persisted.

"Unless you give me complete control of everything, you'll n[ev]er be really fulfilled in this house. Give me the key to the closet, a[nd] if the things I find there fit in with my plans, I'll return them to y[ou.] If not, you'll know that I have something much better for you."

"OK," she said. "I commit my entire home and everything i[n] to you." And as Amber said yes to the designer, she immediately [ex]perienced a genuine peace that she'd never known before.

After that, Amber and the designer had a long talk. He ex-plained that they would always need to be open and honest with each other. "As we walk together I'll show you the things you nee[d] to get rid of or rearrange in your home to make it a better place t[o] live," he said. "And as I show you these things, it will be your re-sponsibility to give them to me."

"I understand," Amber said. "And I promise that I will—wit[h] your help."

"In short," said the designer, "you need to let me redesign y[our] entire home, to redecorate it, and clean it as I see fit—believing th[at] *I* want your happiness even more than *you* do."

Amber listened attentively as he continued. "The changes I make in your home will be for your benefit. For instance, instead [of] spending all your time in the gym, pool, and game room, how about helping fix up several of the spare rooms for strangers who may need a place to stay?"

"Strangers?" Amber said.

"Don't worry," he responded. "I'll help you make wise deci-sions. I'm not talking about letting just *anyone* pop in here. I'm co[m]mitted to your safety. But I know a 17-year-old who's an unwed mother. She's a good kid, but she messed up and doesn't have an[y] where to go."

Amber nodded her head. "I'd love to help."

"And I know a seventh-grader," he continued, "who's being

abused by her stepfather. She feels alone and frightened. I'd love to introduce you to her."

"Yes," Amber said, her eyes filling with tears. "I understand. You want me to be Jesus to those around me—don't you?"

The designer's eyes twinkled. Amber reached inside her purse and pulled out her keys. "Here," she said. "You designed it. You built it. You now own it. I'll continue to live here—but I want you in charge."

The designer put his arm around Amber's shoulders and gave her a tight squeeze. Even though her key ring was now empty, her heart was full. For she knew the designer would be able to do things with the house she'd never before dreamed possible.

## What About You?

Do you need to give the Master Designer control of your house? Maybe you've already asked Him to come inside your house. (In other words, you've invited Jesus into your life.) And that was a good decision. You've noticed a positive difference. Maybe even those around you, like Amber's neighbors, have seen some changes in your life. But perhaps you haven't really given Him total control. When it really comes down to it, who's in charge of your life? You or God?

You see, simply acknowledging that Jesus is real isn't enough. Even Satan does that. And simply praying a quick prayer and inviting Him into your home, or life, isn't enough either. To be a disciple of Jesus Christ means to be saturated with Him. It means giving up your rights and your will. And it means living a holy life.

*But how can I be holy?* you may be thinking. *I'm human! I'm not perfect like Jesus.* That's true. But He can perfect your heart. He can sanctify your will. He can fill you with the power of His Holy Spirit, cleansing you from deep within. And *in His power,* you can live a holy life.

*Does that mean I'll never blow it again?* No. You're human. You'll still fail once in a while. But the difference is that your will—that stubborn, selfish will you were born with—will be committed to

Him. Your deepest desire, therefore, will *not* be to run your own life, call your own shots, or do your own thing. Your greatest desire will be to follow Him in every single area of your life.

You see, Jesus Christ can't settle for being number one in your life, because eventually whatever is number one will be pushed to number two. Jesus doesn't even want the most important spot in your life. *He wants your life!* Understand the difference?

We're not talking about reading your Bible every once in a while, being a good person, going to Sunday School, or being involved in your youth group. Those are great—but anyone can do those things. We're talking about a *lifestyle* change. Being so in love with Jesus that He's the first thing you think about when you wake up in the morning and the last thing on your mind when you fall asleep at night. *Saturated* by Him. *Obsessed* with becoming all He wants you to be. *Totally committed!*

It breaks down like this:

- As a growing Christian obedient to God, acknowledge that you need His cleansing and controlling power released in your life by the Holy Spirit.
- Turn everything over to God. Pray, *Lord, I consecrate myself to You. I want You to completely control my life. ALL of it. From now on.*
- Ask God to release His Spirit in you to cleanse you from sinfulness and to give you power to live a sanctified life.
- Accept God's promised gift to you—His sanctifying Holy Spirit.

- Live each day open to the Holy Spirit's direction and help.

- Tell others what God's Spirit is doing in your life and what He can do in theirs.

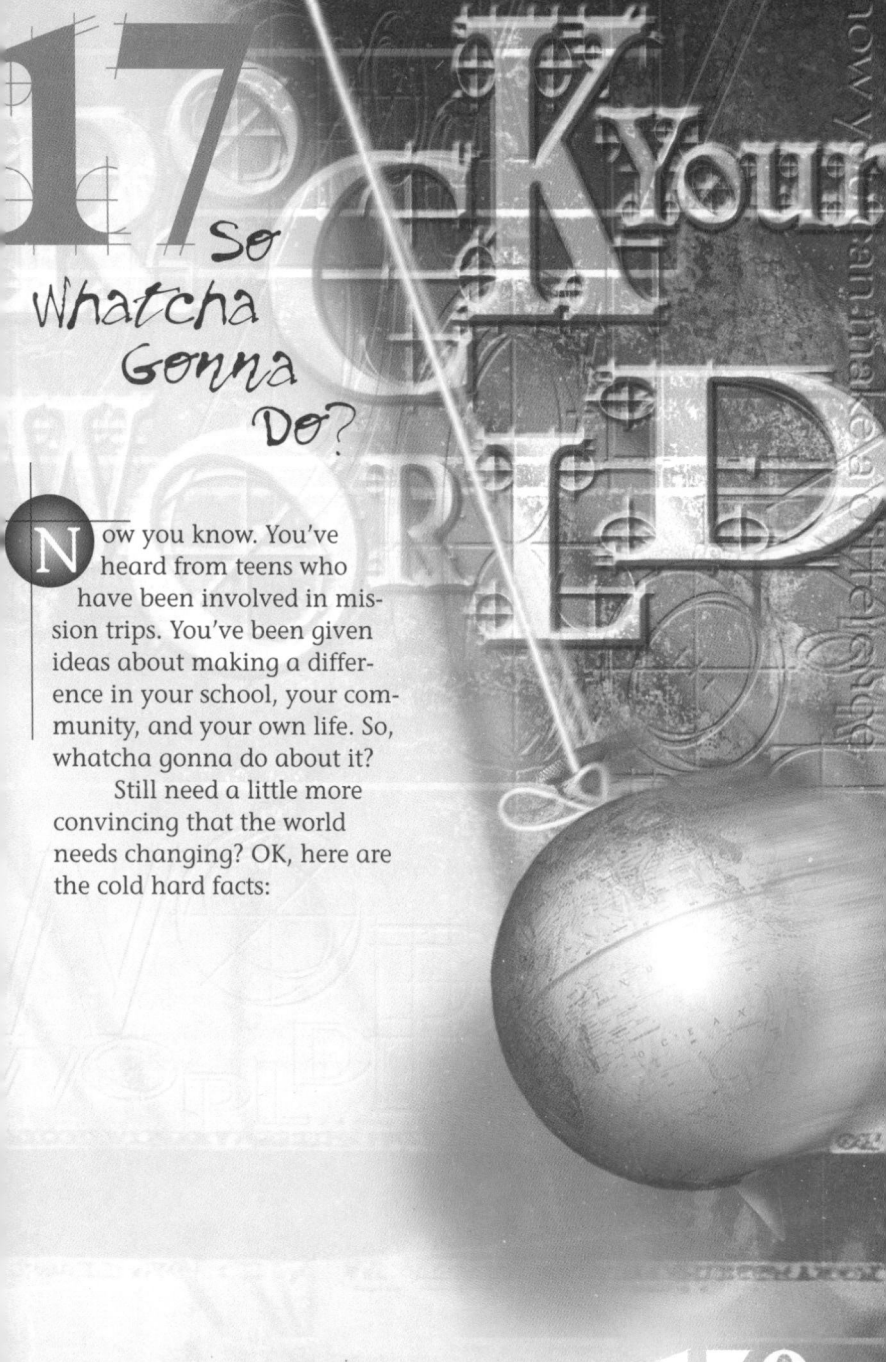

# 17

## So Whatcha Gonna Do?

# ROCK Your WORLD

**N**ow you know. You've heard from teens who have been involved in mission trips. You've been given ideas about making a difference in your school, your community, and your own life. So, whatcha gonna do about it?

Still need a little more convincing that the world needs changing? OK, here are the cold hard facts:

# The Persecuted Church

Unfortunately, Christians are persecuted all over the world simply for what they believe. According to the United States State Department, Christians in over 60 countries face the realities of rape, massacre, family division, torture, mutilation, harassment, imprisonment, slavery, discrimination in education and employment, and even death.

The term "persecuted Church" refers to the worldwide body of people who have chosen Jesus Christ as Lord and leader of their lives. "Persecuted" refers to suffering similar to the situations listed above.

## It's Not New

Persecution of Christians is nothing new; in fact, it can be traced all the way back to the very beginning of Christianity. Jesus Christ himself was martyred on the Cross, and the Early Church faced widespread persecution. While Jesus was on earth, He was a firsthand witness to the battle between God's kingdom and the temporal kingdoms of earth. He told His followers that this tension would sometimes result in physical harm, discrimination, and even death for believers. Jesus said: "'No servant is greater than his master.' If they persecuted me, they will persecute you also" (John 15:20).

Modern-day persecution is well documented. In fact, It's estimated that more Christians were martyred in the 20th century than in the prior 1,900 years combined.

The Bible says that all followers of Jesus Christ should expect persecution (2 Timothy 3:12). Persecution is evil. It is a sin that should be denounced. And while throughout history Christianity has grown tremendously after periods of persecution, we need to keep in mind that this isn't always the case.

# Some of the Stories

- Fifteen-year-old Yaqoob Masih, a Pakistani Christian, died on June 27, 2002, from being tortured by police. He had just started his job as a sweeper for the Customs Department of the government of Pakistan and witnessed an act of bribery between customs officers and the owner of a vehicle who wasn't paying taxes. Yaqoob was warned not to tell senior customs officials what had happened, but he said as a Christian, he'd have to tell the truth if asked. The police tortured and beat Yaqoob severely. Yaqoob passed out due to the excruciating pain, was taken to the hospital, and later died.

- Being a Christian in Pakistan means watching every action, being aware of each spoken word, and tuning in to each glance from another person. Anything said against the prophet of Islam can land a Christian in jail. In fact, false charges are often brought against Christians simply because some of them are better businessmen than a fellow Muslim. Augustine Masih was born into a Christian family and later converted to Islam because he wanted better treatment. In his early adult years, though, he realized his mistake and returned to Christianity. This angered the Muslims in his village, and they accused Augustine of saying blasphemous things about the prophet of Islam. A mob of 200 armed Muslims stormed Augustine's village, and he was taken into custody and charged under blasphemy law. He was sentenced to death and is awaiting his death by hanging.

# Snapshots of a Few Countries

- Afghanistan. The Taliban forces that had been in control of the central government have largely been overthrown by the United States invasion, yet many of the local villages are still run by Taliban forces. This group has established a fundamentalist regime based on their interpretation of Islamic law. There are 48,000 mosques in Afghanistan and not one church building. This country is one of the least-reached nations in the world. Afghanistan is 99.9 percent Muslim, and non-Muslims are denied freedom of assembly. Open profession of Christian faith has often led to death. If you haven't read *Prisoners of Hope: The Story of Our Captivity and Freedom in Afghanistan* by Dayna Curry and Heather Mercer, grab a copy today.

- China. Communism rules this country and continues to inhibit free religious expression. China does have state-sanctioned churches—the Catholic Patriotic Association and the Protestant Three-Self Patriotic Movement—but their actions are tightly controlled by the government. This is why many Christians opt to meet in home churches or "underground" assemblies—they desire the freedom to praise and worship Christ in a more personal way.

- Egypt. Even though Egyptian Christians are beaten and discriminated against, they refuse to talk about it. They believe by keeping quiet, their silence may slightly improve their chances of obtaining a permit from the Egyptian president to operate their religious facilities. This permit is required for anything and everything from building a church to repairing a toilet. Egyptian Christians have

rock your world

been attacked by Muslim extremists without warning. There are reports of Christian girls being abducted, raped, and forced to convert to Islam. Terrorists commonly attack churches and kill Christians.

**Saudi Arabia.** Any expression of Christian worship in this country is forbidden, yet Saudi Arabia demands the right to expand Islam in countries around the world—including the United States—where it finances the building of Islamic academies. No church buildings, crosses, or any religion besides Islam are tolerated. Christians can't even worship privately in their own homes. Islamic police seek out secret worship services by raiding homes. The punishment for Christians if caught in worship? Lengthy imprisonment without trial, torture, and in some cases, death.

**Sudan.** This country has been described by some Christians as a "human hell" because of the rampant torture of believers. Sudan is enduring a seemingly endless civil war and is also being devastated by a jihad led by the militant Islamic regime in Khartoum. Their tactics include aerial bombing of citizens, scorched earth and destruction of livestock, forced displacement of more than 3,000,000 people, imprisonment, torture, execution of men, and abduction and enslavement of women and children.

**North Korea.** Christians being held in North Korean prison camps are special targets of persecution. They are deprived of rest, told to recant, beaten, and assigned the most difficult and dangerous job in the camp. Many, singing hymns as they are beaten, are taken to the electric treatment room where they are tortured and killed. Other Christians in the prison camps have been killed by special death squads and, with molten iron, poured out in a furnace. Along with all of North Korea's people, Christians are also suffering from a devastating famine and face starvation.

# Some of the Stats

- Every night approximately 950 million go hungry.
  *What can you do to make a difference? Give up a couple of pizzas a month, maybe?*

- The Muslim religion is increasing faster than any other major religion, largely due to the high birth rate. For every 1 million Muslims, there is only one missionary available to reach them.
  *The fields are ripe. God needs more laborers. Are you willing?*

- The world is young—with over one-third of the world's population being younger than age 15.
  *What an opportunity to make a difference! As a teenager, you have the best opportunity to reach people your age.*

- Most people make a decision for Christ before they reach the age of 20.
  *God's call is urgent! Time is running out. Are you spreading the Good News?*

- Each year, approximately 3 million children die due to vaccine-prevented diseases, with the same number remaining permanently crippled.
  *We have the cure, the medicines, and the ability. We just don't have enough workers. Pray for God to send more laborers.*

- Approximately 620 million children don't attend school, and half of these do not attend because they don't have access to a school.
  *Have you ever thought about teaching overseas?*

The United States claims 6 percent of the world's population, and yet 94 percent of the world's pastors reside in the States.
*Would you consider ministering overseas?*

Out of the approximate 160,000 people that die every day, 66,000 are unreached people.
*People are dying without even HEARING about Jesus!*

There are 5,103 languages in the world. The Bible has only been translated (in part) into 1,685 of these languages. Yet, there are 36 English translations of the Bible.
*Don't take yours for granted! Use it! Saturate yourself with it!*

## What You Can Do

When faced with stories of persecuted Christians, you may feel hopeless. But your prayers can make all the difference. Consider joining in on the International Day of Prayer for the Persecuted Church (IDOP). It's a global day of intercession for persecuted Christians around the world. This special day is usually the first Sunday in November. Check with your pastor about plans to pray for the persecuted Christians.

### Interruption 4

Turn to page 159 for a list of Scripture passages that talk about persecution.

God calls *all* of us to make a difference. How we do it will vary. Some of you will be called to be medical missionaries. Some will be led to become missionary pilots, accountants, librarians, or song evangelists. God will use some of you in the inner city or with gangs or abused children. Others will be nudged to work in international radio, computers, or film. Some will be called to teach, nurse, preach, write, or act.

## Interruption 5
## Who Will Go?

**Page 160 lists a private conversation between God and a teenager. Check it out. You might just learn something.**

The call for each of us may be different—but we're *all* called. So, whatcha gonna do?

It was he who gave some to be apostles, some to be prophets, some to be evangelists, and some to be pastors and teachers, to prepare God's people for works of service, so that the body of Christ may be built up until we all reach unity in the faith and in the knowledge of the Son of God and become mature, attaining to the whole measure of the fullness of Christ *(Ephesians 4:11-13)*.

Jesus went through all the towns and villages, teaching in their synagogues, preaching the good news of the kingdom and healing every disease and sickness. When he saw the crowds, he had compassion on them, because they were harassed and helpless, like sheep without a shepherd. Then he said to his disciples, "The harvest is plentiful but the workers are few. Ask the Lord of the harvest, therefore, to send out workers into his harvest field" *(Matthew 9:35-38).*

He who has ears to hear, let him hear *(Mark 4:9).*

*Are you listening?*

# Interruptions

## Interruption 1

### Write It Down!

Ready to put your commitment on paper? If you've just made a pledge to stand in the gap, I encourage you to sign this gap pledge card. Then cut it out and put it someplace where you'll see it throughout your day—inside your locker, on your dashboard, on your dresser, or your light switch.

And every time you see this card, let it be a constant reminder that it's OK to endure hardship—expect it. Jesus sure suffered as He hung on the Cross. But also be reminded that you never stand alone!

------------------------------- Cut Here -------------------------------

---

Through **radical** obedience to Jesus Christ,

I **unequivocally** choose to stand in the gap.

This is not a **one-time** commitment;

it's a **lifetime** pledge.

Jesus, use me to be the **bridge**

between a lost world and eternal life.

And, Father,

make my life **forever** different

because of this sacred **covenant**.

---

Your signature

In case you're wondering about that word "unequivocally," it means leading to only one conclusion. And that's how single-minded your gap commitment needs to be. It's as if you're saying, "Father, this pledge will take precedent over everything else in my life. It is my intense focus—no other option. No side-tracking."

# Interruption 2

Check out this fiction story for a fun way that two ordinary teens made a difference in their community. You might get some ideas of your own!

*by Nina Coombs Pykare*

*Keeping the earth clean is a big task. Could two ordinary girls really make a difference?*

We all know moms can get off on tangents sometimes. Take mine. I mean, she has this thing about the environment. My friend Stacy threw her gum wrapper out the car window . . . *just once.* Mom stopped the car right there on Main Street and made her get out and pick it up. Stacy didn't talk to me for a whole week! She was really mad.

Mom kept telling us the earth was our responsibility. That seemed like a pretty big job for one family, but we did our best. Our garage was stuffed with cans and bottles and newspapers for recycling. To give you an idea how far she's willing to go—my mom even recycles junk mail. Every other Saturday we make a trip to the recycling center. Dad says they know us by name.

I didn't care if Mom wanted to clean the house with natural substances. And I even got used to our dog smelling like the garlic she fed it to keep off the fleas.

If you would've asked *me*, I'd have said there wasn't one more single solitary thing our family could do to protect the environment. But naturally I was wrong.

## One More Thing

When the new baby came, things got even worse. I mean, how many mothers do you know who *refuse* to use disposable diapers?

I heard Mom explain it to Aunt Susan one day. "Disposable diapers aren't disposable," Mom said with that light in her eye. "They aren't biodegradable, and they trap and breed germs for years and years."

Aunt Susan wasn't buying. "But the work they save," she said. "And the mess."

The glint in Mom's eyes grew fiercer. "We're going to have an even bigger mess if we don't stop. Do you know that in this country alone we use enough of those diapers every year to fill a football field 30 stories high? *In one year!*"

Aunt Susan didn't look impressed, but Beth woke up from her nap and started to cry, so I went to get her. Of course her pants were full.

I changed her and set her on the bathroom floor while I washed out her dirty diaper in the toilet. She laughed and made kissing noises at me, but it was still a smelly job. I had to agree with Aunt Susan. It would be so much easier just to wrap the whole thing up and throw it away.

Afterward, I put Beth in her playpen and went down to the cellar to get the last load of diapers. All of our chores were rearranged after the baby arrived, and you can guess who got the washing-the-diapers job.

## An Understanding Friend

I didn't mind a whole lot, at least not in the summer. But now that it was getting colder, I didn't like hanging them outside. Sure, we've got a dryer. But Mom doesn't believe in wasting gas, either.

That's why, when the new girl moved in next door, I was out hanging diapers—the week before Easter.

Since I'm naturally friendly, I hollered, "Hi."

She meandered over. "Hi. I'm Cassie."

"My name's Tonnie." I saw her looking in the basket. "Diapers," I said. "The kind you have to wash."

"Really?"

"Really. It's my mom's idea."

Cassie stared at me. "I can't believe it."

"Believe what?"

"Your mom."

Now, *I* thought Mom was weird, but I wasn't about to let anyone *else* put her down. "She's a great mom," I defended.

Cassie started to laugh. "Yeah," she said. "So is mine."

"Huh?" I wasn't getting any of this.

"You aren't going to believe it, but your mom is just like mine." I almost sat down right there on the cold grass. I mean, there couldn't possibly be two of them.

Cassie giggled. "Does she stop the car if you throw something out?"

"Are you kidding? Yes!" And I told her about Stacy.

As you can imagine, Cassie and I quickly became friends. So did our moms.

We loved them but were embarrassed by them too. And we were even more humiliated when they decided to go to the town council to propose a ban on disposable diapers.

Mom said, "Maybe you and Cassie would like to come along."

We shook our heads vigorously. "We're just kids," I mumbled. "We can't do anything."

"Sure you can," Cassie's mother said. "Everyone can do something.

Cassie and I just looked at each other. *Mothers! How could you make them understand?*

But after they went to the meeting, Cassie and I both got jumpy. We just couldn't sit still. Finally, I said, "Want to walk over? Just to see what's happening?" She had her coat on before I finished talking.

## Taking a Stand

A lot of people were at the meeting, mostly of the age to have babies. "We were right," I said. "It's never going to pass."

Our moms got their chance to speak, and then they opened the floor for questions. With Dad being out of town, I was glad I was there to give Mom moral support.

It didn't take long to get the picture. These people were willing to make the whole earth into a garbage dump if it saved them from handling messy diapers. Cassie and I looked at each other. Our moms might be weird, but we were beginning to think that these people were even *more* weird.

A woman with a sad face got up and said, "You have a good point, but we're just one small town. We can't really change anything."

Before I knew what was happening, I was on my feet. "It's true we're only one small town," I began. "But my mom's only one person, and *she's* making a difference. We can too!" Someone mumbled something, but I rushed on.

"This isn't California where we're in the midst of a water shortage and have plenty of desert space for landfill. We live in Idaho! Wake up, everyone. Disposable diapers are nice—for right now. But we've got to think about later. I don't want *my* babies to grow up in a world that's become a garbage dump. Do you?"

I sat down quickly, sweating and feeling pretty silly. Imagine *me* spouting off in public like that!

Cassie squeezed my arm. "You were great!" she whispered. And up on the stage, I saw Mom dabbing at her eyes and smiling proudly.

## Making a Difference

The council didn't pass the ordinance . . . we hadn't really expected it would. Yet. But we didn't intend to be quitters.

Cassie and I put our heads together and started a "Save the Earth" club at church. We made pledge cards and asked everyone with babies to pledge not to use disposable diapers. At first it was scary, asking people something like that. But after we pointed out the facts, some of the parents signed the pledge. And even those who didn't, looked a little concerned—like they'd at least think about it.

Next, we sent teams of kids door-to-door to explain the problem and ask people to sign petitions to ban disposable diapers in our town. We got *hundreds* of signatures.

When our school principal heard about what we were doing, he asked us to speak to all the classes.

We took surveys to see how many babies there were in the school families and how many diapers they'd be using. Then kids went home with the facts. When some of the parents realized how serious the students were, they quit using disposables!

In a couple of months, the council will vote again. This time we think we have enough public opinion to get the ordinance passed. But if we don't, we'll just keep at it. We figure we're on our way to preventing at least a *few* stories of this year's 30-story high football field.

Sometimes Cassie and I look at each other and laugh. Here we are, acting every bit as weird as our moms. But now that doesn't matter. Because, well when the earth's your responsibility, you've got to take care of it.

*"Just Kids," by Nina Coombs Pykare first appeared in the 1993 April issue of* Brio *magazine.*

*Just How Wide IS Your Worldview? Let's Find Out!*

The Cross-Cultural Connection: Test Your Global Perspective!
*How do you rate when it comes to knowing, understanding, and appreciating different cultures and people? Take this quiz to find out if you're "culturally connected," or if you need to get your head out of the sand!*

1. If given a choice to travel, you'd choose:
   a. France.
   b. Disney World.
   c. The mall.

2. Your mom's encouraging you to spend a year abroad as a foreign exchange student. Your reaction:
   a. Where's the plane ticket?
   b. Sounds like a good experience.
   c. What? And miss a year of "Survivor?"

3. Your dad gets reassigned to another country. Your family is moving in two weeks, and you feel:
   a. totally gung-ho.
   b. kinda nervous.
   c. banished into exile.

4. Your youth group is planning a mission trip to Costa Rica. After reading the information packet, you decide:
   a. you can't wait to pack.
   b. you'll consider it if your friends go.
   c. you'd rather make money flipping burgers.

5. Your best friend calls to tell you about a great opportunity to write an international pen pal. You:
   a. jump at the chance.
   b. tell her you'll think about it.
   c. say "no thanks" right away.

6. An ad in a magazine asks for your support of a needy child in an underdeveloped country. You think:
   a. *That's something I'd really like to do.*
   b. *It's worth looking into.*
   c. *No way would I waste my money on that!*

7. There are five international students at your school this year. You:
   a. know all five on a first-name basis.
   b. would like to get to know them but aren't sure how to introduce yourself.
   c. have no idea who they are or where they're from.

8. You pray for people in other countries:
   a. regularly.
   b. once in a while.
   c. never even thought about it.

# Scoring:

If you answered *mostly A's,* you've made the cross-cultural connection! You're not afraid to step out of your own comfort zone, and you're an international risk-taker who likes to pursue getting to know other cultures, languages, and people. Keep up the good work!

If you answered *mostly B's,* it's the right time to get moving! You're headed in the right direction, but you need to push yourself a little more to explore other cultures and customs. Don't be afraid! When meeting people from other countries, concentrate on trying to make *them* feel comfortable. Take a risk! You'll be glad you did.

If you answered *mostly C's,* you're wearing cultural blinders! Sadly, you're missing incredible opportunities to enrich your life by exposing yourself to other cultures and people. After all, there's more to life than TV and the mall! God created an amazing variety of people and places—get to know some!

*This quiz by Sara Meekhof was first printed in the August 1997 issue of* Brio *magazine.*

# Interruption 4:
## Scriptures on Persecution

The Bible has a lot to say about persecution and the battle waged between the kingdom of God and the forces of this world. Familiarize yourself with the following Scriptures, and ask God to help you understand the grace we are given as we identify with Jesus Christ through suffering.

Scriptures that address persecution:

Exodus 4—7
Job 19:25
Psalm 115:6
119:161-162
Proverbs 24:11-12
Isaiah 52:13
Matthew 5:11-12
5:43-48
6:5-15
10:38-42
27:19-60
Mark 8:31-38
14:65
16:1-20
Luke 6:27-36
14:25-35
15:16-20
18:1-8
21:12-14
22:47-54
24:39-43

John 13:16
14:1-4
15:16-20
16:2
16:22
16:33
19:28-37
Acts 12:5
Romans 8:17-37
12:14
1 Corinthians 1:18-31
4:12
12:2, 12
2 Corinthians 1:1-12
3:12-18
4:7-17
6:1-10
11:16-30
Galatians 6:9-10, 17
Ephesians 4:1-6

Philippians 1:28-29
3:9-10
Colossians 4:18
2 Thessalonians 1:4
2:13-15
1 Timothy 2:1-2
2 Timothy 1:8
3:12
Hebrews 10:19-39
13:3
James 1:1-4
5:7-20
1 Peter 2:13-25
3:8-18
4:12-19
Revelation 2:8-17
3:7-13
6:10
20:4
21:12

# Interruption 5
## Who Will Go?

*God Said . . . I Said*

*This is private. DON'T READ! (Unless you enjoy eavesdropping.)*

**He Said:** I'm looking for a teen girl who will follow Me.

**I Said:** I will, Lord. In fact, I already am.

**Really? How?**

Well, I go to church. And Sunday School too!

**A lot of people do that.**

Yeah, but I also read the Bible. In fact, I even have one of those cool student versions!

**That's great. But that's also easy—doesn't take much effort. In fact, sometimes I wonder why you even do it.**

Well, it helps me to know what others are doing wrong.

**I see.**

And reading the Bible makes me feel good.

**Oh. Is that important? That you *feel good*?**

Well, yeah. Because if I'm following You, I should *feel* good about it.

**Hmmm.**

Think about it, Lord. If it didn't *feel* good, it would be hard to get others to come to You. That's why our youth group has so many cool activities—'cause it *feels good* to have a beach party and bike hikes and video nights. Think I could ever get anyone to come if it wasn't something that felt *good*?

**So, you're a Christian because it feels good?**

Well, heaven will feel good. And that's *definitely* where I wanna end up. So yeah, I guess feeling good is a big part of my relationship with You.

**I'm looking for a teen who will follow Me.**

I will, Lord. In fact, I *am* following You.

**Are you following ME? Or are you following your feelings?**

Well, um, You. I mean, I . . . uh . . .

**I'm looking for a teen who will follow Me in the good times and in the bad times.**

Well, Lord, don't forget that I, uh . . .

**Someone who will follow Me no matter WHAT the cost.**

Hey, God. This is getting weird.

**A teen who will devote her LIFE to Me.**

Whoa. Sounds like 100 percent.

**Someone who will make Me her top priority.**

You're Number One. Hey! You're Number One. Hey!

**A teen who will love ME more than anything and anyone else in her life.**

So You didn't like my little Number One cheer, huh? Lord, I love You more than anyone else.

**And someone who won't call me "Lord" unless I truly am.**

It's Todd Washington, isn't it? That's what You're getting at. I can't help it, God, I've liked Todd for three years. Now that we're finally getting together, well, Todd's all I can think about. And You're saying You want me to think about YOU more than Todd Washington? This is Todd Washington, God. *Todd Washington!*

**I know. I created Todd, remember?**

Well, OK then. You should know how important this relationship is to me. And how important *lots* of relationships are to me right now.

**I'm looking for a teen who will follow Me. Someone who will commit her *life* to Me. A teen who will truly make Me LORD, of every area in her life.**

God, this isn't how You want to run an advertising campaign. Sèe, You've got it all backward. If You want people to follow You, You have to make it sound attractive.

**Someone who will pick up her cross and follow Me.**

That's *not* attractive, God. You'd probably get more response if You said something like, "I'm looking for someone who'll stand in the spotlight and sing for Me." Or how 'bout "Someone who'll be on TV and act for Me." See, you have to make it *sound* good to catch people's attention. This thing with the Cross, well, it's just not a good hook.

**Someone who's not following Me for riches or fame or feel-good emotions. I need a teen who will literally DIE to what *she* wants and who will accept *My* plan for her instead.**

Ah, God. There You go with the unattractive stuff again. Are You listening? I'm trying to help You come up with a creative advertising approach—something that will bring people to You in droves!

**Do you think Abraham felt good about placing his only son on a sacrificial altar?**

Hmmm. I must have missed that Sunday.

**Or that it felt good to many of the early Christians to be tortured?**

Well, we *say* tortured. But we can't really know for sure what happened back then. We just can't go assuming—

**Open your Bible.**

My Bible? Well, it's not really time for my devotions, God. See, I usually don't read the Bible until I'm almost asleep.

**Open your Bible to Hebrews chapter 11. Start with verse 36.**

*(Sigh.)* OK. "Some were laughed at and their backs cut open with whips, and others were chained in dungeons. Some died by stoning and some by being sawed in two" (TLB). This is gross.

**It certainly didn't *feel* good, did it? I'm looking for a teen girl who will love ME more than her own life.**

You're asking a lot, God.

**What's it say about Noah?**

Says he trusted You even though there wasn't any sign of a flood.

**And how do you think people around him reacted?**

Ha! They probably thought he was a mental case. I mean, up to this point in history they'd never even *seen* rain, right? The earth was simply watered by the dew.

**Think it *felt good* to be laughed at?**

Well . . .

**Yet he continued to follow Me. What's it say about Joseph?**

Uh, let's see. Oh, here it is—verse 22. It says he was faithful.

**Think it *felt good* to be abandoned by his family, spend time in prison for a crime he didn't commit, and live in another culture? It took him years even to figure out the language!**

I never thought about that.

**And what does it say about Sarah?**

Here it is. Verse 11. Says she trusted You. That even in her old age, she believed You'd keep Your word about blessing her with a child.

**Do you think it *felt good* when others mocked her for expecting a child when she was a senior citizen?**

Hmmm.

**I'm not looking for followers who will stand by Me when it *feels good*. I know that kind of commitment at best is only surface and temporary. I'm searching *desperately* for someone who will follow Me *no matter what the cost!***

Those are high stakes, God.

**I'm combing all of Earth to find her—that one teen who will give Me her entire life. Because you see, all I need is *one life* completely sold out to Me, to My plan, to My will—*one life*, and I can impact the *world!***

I've never been much at taking risks, God.

**One teen who will say, "Here I am, Lord. Use me. If You want me to sing, I'll sing. If You want to send me to a foreign land, I'll go. If You want me to speak up in school, I will. *Whatever* You ask, I'll do."**

To be real honest, God. I don't know of *anyone* who would answer *that* kind of invitation. I mean, after all, we wouldn't even know what to say or what to do.

**Look at Jeremiah 1:4-9 (TLB). What's it say?**

Well, it starts off with a conversation between You and him. You're good at these one-on-ones, aren't You?

**I *invented* speaking, remember?**

It says that You appointed Jeremiah as Your spokesman. I'm assuming that means You wanted him to speak out for You. And with the way *our* conversation is going, that probably means to speak out in a bold way—when it was convenient and when it wasn't, right? Like, it wouldn't always *feel good* to do it?

**You're catching on.**

But it looks as though Jeremiah had a few excuses. He goes, "'O Lord God,' I said. 'I can't do that! I'm far too young! I'm only a youth!'"

And You know, God, I think I have to agree—

**Keep reading.**

*(Sigh.)* Well, then You answered him. "'Don't say that,' he [You] replied, 'for you will go wherever I send you and speak whatever I tell you to.'" This is where I need to help You understand what it's like today, God. See, if I spoke out for You in class or in the cafeteria or in the locker room, well, people would make fun of me!

**Read on.**

"'And don't be afraid of the people, for I, the Lord, will be with you and see you through.'" Well, maybe so. But if *I* were Jeremiah . . . I mean if You were asking *me* to speak out for You . . . well, I wouldn't have any idea what to say!

**You're not finished yet.**

OK. Uh, oh yeah. Here we are. "Then he touched my mouth and said, 'See, I have put my words in your mouth!'" Kind of have an answer for everything, don't You, Father?

**Well, I *am* GOD. And the truth is, I'd *never* ask you to do something without equipping you with everything you need in order to do it!**

Now, don't get me wrong, God. I wanna follow You. But I've still got my own life to live, You know?

**Thousands of teens will read the book you're holding. I'm just looking for *one* who will say, "I'm Yours, Lord. Break me and reshape me into Your image. I want nothing more than Your perfect will to be done in my life."**

Maybe thousands will read this book. And maybe most of them will even eavesdrop on our conversation. But thousands of teens are not going to jump to *this* kind of invitation. I'm telling You, God, You gotta create a better publicity program.

I'm not looking for thousands. I started with 12, remember? I'm looking for *one*. One. That's all I need. One who will pick up the cross and follow Me. One who would be willing to spend some time in another country helping those less fortunate than himself. Or who would give sacrificially so a little child could be fed and schooled. Someone who would put aside his own desires of *feel-good* plans and say instead, "Use Me, Father. Use Me."

*"Then I heard the Lord asking, 'Whom shall I send as a messenger to my people? Who will go?'*
*"And I said, 'Lord, I'll go! Send **me**'"* (Isaiah 6:8, TLB).

# About the author . . .

Susie Shellenberger is editor of the popular girls' magazine, *BRIO*. She's a former youth pastor and high school teacher who has been to every continent in the world leading thousands of teenagers on mission trips. Susie also cohosts the nationally syndicated *Life on the Edge Live* radio program and has written numerous books for teens.

To schedule Susie Shellenberger to speak for your group, contact the Ambassador Agency: 615-370-4700.